ITALIAN POETRY TODAY:

CURRENTS AND TRENDS

an anthology

edited

by

Ruth Feldman & Brian Swann

With an Introduction by Glauco Cambon

New Rivers Press

1979

Copyright © 1979 by New Rivers Press
Library of Congress Catalog Card Number: 7963481
ISBN 0-89823-003-9
All Rights Reserved
Book Design: C.W. Truesdale
Typography: Michael Labriole

ITALIAN POETRY TODAY has been published with the aid of supporting grants from the National Endowment for the Arts and the New York State Council on the Arts.

New Rivers Press Books are distributed by:
        SBD: Small Press Distribution
        Jeanetta Jones Miller
        1636 Ocean View Avenue
        Kensington, California 94707

ITALIAN POETRY TODAY has been manufactured in the United States of America for New Rivers Press (C.W. Truesdale, Editor/Publisher), 1602 Selby Avenue, St. Paul, Minnesota 55104 in a first edition of 2000 copies.

EDITORS' FOREWORD

We originally intended this anthology to be devoted exclusively to 'younger' poets. But it soon became clear that such a limitation would be artificial and of limited value. What about poets who began writing poetry later in life? As Giovanni Cecchetti wrote to us, concerning the novelist Vasco Pratolini: "I am convinced that the ages of poets cannot be computed on the basis of their birth certificates."

Yet we did retain other limitations. We wanted poets who were less well-known in this country, for instance. This meant that we chose, reluctantly, not to include such important poets as Luzi, Zanzotto, Cattafi, Giudice, Sereni, and others who have been published in book form here, or in large selections. A larger, more comprehensive anthology would, of course, have to include these poets, and others. Since we had to work within the limitations of a certain number of pages, however, space was at a premium. Where there was competition between a more established poet and an interesting less well-known one, we opted for the latter.

It was our wish, then, to introduce new voices, some of which haven't been heard very frequently in Italy itself. We also felt that English-speaking readers would be interested in hearing a poet of note like Pasolini in translations from his native Friulan. This particular selection is included as a tribute to a man of genius whose life was brutally shortened.

Doubtless there are idiosyncracies in our choices. Doubtless, too, there is evidence of ignorance. But we would like to think that the choices, if idiosyncratic, are not cranky, and if there is ignorance, it is honest ignorance. In passing, it might be noted that some poets we wished to include are not represented because of the inability of their translators to meet our deadline.

A brief note on method. Some poems were sent in unsolicited. Others were chosen by the editors, and translators were asked to work on them. We would like to thank all the translators who, with their skill and generosity, made this anthology possible, and who took the editors' suggestions in good part.

We would also like to express gratitude to Marco Forti, of Arnoldo Mondadori Editore for his extensive support and assistance, and to the publishing house itself. We also thank Luigi Ballerini for helping us to contact poets and for supplying the art work used in this book. Acknowledgements are due to the publications where some of these poems first appeared: *Durak, Granite, Mediterranean Review, Modern Poetry in Translation, The Penguin Book of Women Poets, Translation.*

Brian Swann and Ruth Feldman

ITALIAN POETRY TODAY

9.	Introduction By Glauco Cambon
14.	Key To Translators' Initials
17.	Nanni Balestrini
20.	Luigi Ballerini
23.	Dario Belleza
26.	Piero Bigongiari
28.	Alfredo Bonazzi
32.	Edith Bruck
36.	Ferdinando Camon
38.	Giorgio Caproni
40.	Giovanni Cecchetti
43.	Guido Ceronetti
45.	Giorgio Chiesura
48.	Pietro Cimatti
52.	Elena Clementelli
55.	Roberto Coppini
57.	Raffaele Crovi
59.	Maurizio Cucchi
64.	Brandolino Brandolini d'Adda
66.	Milo De Angelis
68.	Alfredo De Palchi
71.	Arnaldo Di Benedetto
74.	Luciano Erba
77.	Elizabeth Ferrero
80.	Gilberto Finzi
83.	Andrea Genovese
87.	Amedeo Giacomini
89.	Alfredo Giuliani
93.	Renato Gorgoni
95.	Margherita Guidacci
98.	Armanda Guiducci
100.	Federico Hindermann
102.	Gina Labriola
106.	Mario Lunetta
108.	Giorgio Luzzi
109.	Giancarlo Majorino

113.	Giorgio Manacorda
118.	Giorgio Mannacio
120.	Dacia Maraini
124.	Elsa Morante
128.	Alberto Mario Moriconi
134.	Giampiero Neri
137.	Giulia Niccolai
140.	Stanislao Nievo
143.	Rossana Ombres
147.	Giorgio Orelli
150.	Elio Pagliarani
154.	Pier Paolo Pasolini
157.	Camillo Pennati
161.	Allesandro Peregalli
164.	Danilo Plateo
166.	Antonio Porta
170.	Vasco Pratolini
173.	Giovanni Raboni
177.	Silvio Ramat
180.	Franco Rella
182.	Nelo Risi
185.	Roberto Roversi
189.	Sergio Salvi
192.	Giovanna Sandri
195.	Roberto Sanesi
198.	Edoardo Sanguineti
203.	Francesco Smeraldi
204.	Adriano Spatola
212.	Maria Luisa Spaziani
215.	David M. Turoldo
217.	Carlo Villa
219.	Cesare Vivaldi
220.	Paolo Volponi
224.	Notes
225.	Biographical Notes On The Poets
232.	Biographical Notes On The Translators

ART WORK

cover, Emilio Villa, *Idrologie*
2. Patricia Vicinelli, *Poesia*
16. Eugenio Miccini, *Poesia, Gloria e Tragedia*
35. Claudio Parmiggiani, *Tavola Analfabetica*
51. Giovanna Sandri, *Tantra*
73. Emilio Isgrò, *Poesia Volkswagen*
112. Vincenzo Accame, *Prova de circolarita'*
160. Sandri, *AA Galaxy OP 238, 738*
176. Luciano Caruso, *De Inventione Linguarum*
222-3. Gianni Emilio Simonetti, *For Sixtem Arches*

Glauco Cambon

INTRODUCTION

It takes courage to venture into a partly uncharted wilderness, and this is what my old friends Ruth Feldman and Brian Swann have done in making their selections for the present anthology of recent Italian verse. Leaving behind, not only the Founding Fathers generation of by now amply recognized twentieth-century figures like Ungaretti and Montale, or Campana (who was so diligently translated by I.L. Salomon), but also the subsequent generation centered on "Hermeticists" like Quasimodo, Betocchi, Gatto, Luzi or Sereni (and here again, we should remember I.L. Solomon's and Allen Mandelbaum's pioneering work), Swann and Feldman are now sampling the work of young poets, many of them experimental, and some still obscure in their native Italy. In this enterprise, the two anthologists and translators have had a forerunner a few years ago in Frank Judge, who edited a special issue of the *Vanderbilt Poetry Review* entirely devoted to new Italian verse, and who is now also contributing some translations to Swann's and Feldman's anthology. Some of the choices here may also stem from his own (Bonazzi, for instance).

On the other hand, Feldman and Swann have left out some postwar poets of note (Cattafi, Giudici, Zanzotto, Bodini) who appeared in the 1974 *Vanderbilt Poetry Review* selection, as well as in their own special Italian issue of *Modern Poetry in Translation,* no. 26, Winter 1975. One of these (Zanzotto) has been introduced to the English speaking world by Feldman and Swann in a sustained bilingual anthology published by Princeton University Press, and another (Cattafi) has received from them the same kind of attention, the book-length manuscript being now ready for publication. Giudici, who ranks with Zanzotto in his generation, has been translated by Mandelbaum and that book is also awaiting publication with a University press; Bodini's recognition as a significant Southern modernist poet is long overdue outside Italy. While I cannot argue with my friends about their reasons for these and other unignorable exclusions (like Franco Fortini), I should be happier if they had not occurred, since some of these poets' contemporary peers (Erba, Spaziani, Pasolini, Orelli) have been included – and their original appearance dates from the 1954 anthology, *Quarta Generazione* (edited by Erba and Chiara), which also had Cattafi and Zanzotto in its rich pages.

Such reservations, anyhow, are outweighed by the rewards in the present book. Apart from the excellent translations by the joint anthologists themselves and by other experienced hands, the rewards must be seen in the thrill of discovery that the anthology as a whole affords. It is unabashedly offbeat and it lays no claim to completeness or organic representation. It takes real chances, for some of the inclusions are tantamount to wagers; Feldman and Swann refuse to abide by Establishment accolades. Time will tell; but whether further time will show whether they are kingmakers or not, time present already bears witness to their alertness as samplers of manifold voices which can still vibrate, each on its own particular wavelength, as transcribed for a different linguistic instrument. Taken together, these choices give a fair idea of the variety of trends and tempers in the new Italian poetry.

There are to be heard, first of all, the "Fourth Generation" poets who took up the challenge of filling the void left in the immediate postwar years by the demise of the so-called Hermetic dispensation. Some members of this group, like Erba, Orelli, and Spaziani (to mention those who are included in the present selection), chose not to break completely with the tradition of intellectual allusiveness, semantic concentration, verbal fastidiousness and recondite imagery that the dominant poets of the period between the two world wars had established. And in the quarter of a century since their debut in the epoch-making anthology by Erba and Chiara, these supposedly transitional writers have quietly kept up their nonrevolutionary work. Nobody will deny their staying power, or their achieved stylistic physiognomy. Thus Maria Luisa Spaziani has developed along purely lyrical lines, with sustained musical effusiveness in the standard hendecasyllable measure, and concomitant emphasis on striking, often exuberant imagery. Her poetry, whether it takes its cue from a travelogue form or from the diary confession, never ceases to surprise the reader. She simply dares to *sing* — at a time when singing, the lyrical voice, has been about as suspect as operatic *bel canto* in the era of atonal music. Erba's music is more withdrawn, and his imagery far sparer; combined with an irony that marks the questing attitude, and with the flat references to places and people of seeming insignificance, these traits add up to a subtle incisiveness, a piercing individuation of tone. Orelli — whose 1977 book, *Sinopie,* has come to crown an unremitting dedication to the art — likewise becomes memorable through sheer sobriety. The self-effacing style, the understatement, the reliance on unadorned objective detail, convey a feeling of specific reality, of authentic experience, of the thisness of things and moments. Orelli's scenery and creatures are as Italian-Swiss as Erba's are Lombard. Not a cramping regionalism, but a Hopkinsian "instress of inscape" is involved; the realization that meaning can be attained only in the particular, in the here-and-now of the human condition. If such poets are conservative, they are certainly not epigonal.

Conversely, the candid reader's exposure to tortured experimenters like Balestrini, Giuliani, Sanguineti, Porta, and Pagliarani — the writers who boomed their way into public awareness with the *Novissimi* anthology of 1960 and the 1963 gathering of "Gruppo 63" — may well turn out to be traumatic, or at least disconcerting. Here are poets who seem to deny the very essence of what had been considered poetry for so many centuries: verbal melody, self-expressiveness, semantic and syntactical coherence. Free verse, after Whitman, the *Symbolistes* and the Futurists, is of course no novelty, and in fact this postwar Italian avant-garde has harkened back in a few things to Grandpa Marinetti, whose 1909 and 1912 pleas for a total break with the received tradition have echoed forth in the radical program of the *Novissimi,* compounded with a good dose of anti-bourgeois, Marxistically oriented ideology. Pound, Brecht and Eliot supply further ingredients to their aggressive poetics, and the results can be seen in the variously fractured, anti-lyrical, rough and yet intellectually underpinned, at times polyglot idiom(s). Giuliani is the one among them who seems closest to a coherent language with his emphasis on hyperbolic imagery á la Dylan Thomas, while Balestrini works with clever syntactical intarsia, sometimes bordering on visual or concrete poetry, and Sanguineti hammers away at the reader with a kind of highbrow esperanto repeatedly seeking the breakthrough of prophetic utterance (he happens to be a consummate scholar and a fine Dante critic). As for Porta, he depersonalizes language no less than Balestrini, to challenge the habits allegedly instilled in today's readership by what passes for a complacent capitalist taste. With them, the poem ceases to be confession, vision or song, the expression of a self, to become a provocative linguistic object, a destructive "impersonal" construct which is meant to lay bare the unreliable condition of expression and communication in a falsified human world. Pagliarani is something else again, with his cinematographic realism focusing on alienated life in an industrial metropolis. If the *Novissimi*'s flareup in the Sixties has subsided somewhat, in the nature of all iconoclastic movements, they cannot be said to have remained without a following, Adriano Spatola and Luigi Ballerini being the most noteworthy examples. Ballerini's impressive recent texts, which combine photography, philosophical quotations and cryptic utterance, have remained outside the scope of the present anthology, but they amount to a moving testimonial to Ezra Pound's impact on the younger creative minds of the country that was the first and the last to receive the restless American expatriate. Pound's radicalizing influence has made itself variously felt in the other young experimenters gravitating on avant-garde magazines like *Marcatré, Antipiugiú, La battana, Tam Tam.*

The experimental temper has not gone out of Italian poetry; if anything it has been reactivated by the massive spread of structuralist and semiotic studies; Umberto Eco was one of the key figures at the 1963 Palermo meeting that sanctioned the national resonance of what had started out as a tiny group of five avant garde hopefuls gravitating on Luciano Anceschi's *Il Verri* magazine. But apart from the question of whether poetry can be purely polemical, and language build on anti-language, it pays to consider the dialectical space that opens up for us in the polarization between "Fourth Generation" conservatives and "Novissimi" iconoclasts. As far as the assumptions of poetics go, it is within this tense space that all possible phenomena in Italian poetry must be situated in the decades under analysis.

Silvio Ramat, for instance, with his neo-baroque experimentalism, occupies an intermediate position between the Milanese young Turks of *Gruppo 63* and the "Fourth Generation" conservatives whose Hermetic background cannot be denied, since in most cases it has functioned as a springboard. Actually, even one of the pre-war Hermeticists, Florentine Piero Bigongiari, is included in

Feldman's and Swann's selection; he has kept up the endeavor of self-renewal, and one of his last books, *Antimateria* (Anti-matter), shows bold avant-garde traits. Bigongiari, it should be noted, is also an extremely insightful and mercurial essayist; it's hard to separate the poet from the critic in his case. And Pier Paolo Pasolini, whose international reputation as offbeat novelist, neorealist film director and left-wing journalist had steadily grown before his weird murder suddenly placed him for a while in the world's limelight, historically belongs to the "Fourth Generation" group because of his early appearance in the *Quarta Generazione* anthology of verse; but as a poet he is simultaneously right and left of that group. With Roberto Roversi, who is also represented in the selection on hand, he edited for years the periodical *Officina* (Workshop), a forum for literary debate with strong social and political implications; it published the new work of *engagé* writers like himself, and it acquired widespread influence. Now Pasolini, with his populist socialism, was miles apart from the doctrinaire intellectualism of Sanguineti and the rest of the *Novissimi*, and he wrote poetry and prose drawing on the language of the rural and urban disinherited. His interest in folk literature and dialect poetry never flagged, and it led to the editing of an anthology of modern Italian dialect poetry which remains one of his durable contributions to our culture. The Italian verse he produced till the end could be in turn aggressively discursive or narratively syncopated. In all of this, as well as in his muck-raking fiction, he showed a marked experimental temper; but his best achievement must be seen in the Friulano dialect verse which began and concluded his stormy career. No translation, obviously, can ever intimate the piercing sweetness of this music, at once humble and eerily remote, as if a medieval troubadour had returned from the grave to sing again. Pasolini's unique ear for the venerable, if sometimes despised, phenomenon of dialect, is part of his achievement, and the present anthology includes another dialect poet, the Genoese Vivaldi, who stands apart from the literary squabbles to perfect his unmistakable voice. More such poets should have attracted the attention of our two joint anthologists, Franco Loi of Milan, for instance; but at least this particular note is not wanting in the gamut as sampled.

The fury, and the sweetness, that go into the alchemy of verse make themselves heard, in a different proportion, in the work of Pietro Cimatti, a maverick whose love-hate relation to the common Catholic heritage of Italy has eventuated in sharp satire. But his poem on the Day of All Souls transcends satire; the bitterness is but the other side of personal concern. It would be hard to grade or describe the several new voices of Italian poetry along the scale we have set up; the "disaffection" of Cimatti, for instance, next to the affectionate endurance of Bonazzi, whose acquaintance with crime and jail has not stifled, has indeed instigated his poetical vein. They are, in different ways, "absolutely out" (*assolutamente fuori*), to say it in the words of Cimatti's title, and so is — as an outspoken singer of homosexuality — Dario Bellezza, whose non-experimental yet far from reactionary verse achieves a strong individual tone. So is, in still another way, the markedly experimental (and confessional) Alfredo De Palchi, an expatriate with a destiny and a burden — which he knows how to articulate in poignant lines. "Assolutamente fuori" are, in a sense, some of the women poets here sampled: Edith Bruck, for one, with her savage anti-lyricism and her death camp background; Armanda Guiducci, the pugnacious feminist who made a name for herself with a polemical essay on Pavese, and is now showing a gift for sharp imagery; Dacia Maraini, novelist and poet, unconventional woman, one time inmate of Japanese prison camps. As for Stanislao Nievo, descendant of an outstanding Risorgimento writer and warrior, he strikes his own mysterious note, apart from all schools. In short, nearly everybody in the heterogeneous company assembled here seems to be rather "out" than "in." But who is "in" any more? The book registers in effect the crisis of modern poetry in Italian. A crisis can be a good thing. So let us wait and see.

Glauco Cambon. Spring-Summer 1978.

KEY TO TRANSLATORS' INITIALS

WA	William Alexander
KDA	Karen D. Antonelli
JA	John Ashbery
AB	Anita Barrows
PB	Peter Burian
GC	Giovanni Cecchetti
MJC	Mary Jane Ciccarello
AD	Ann Deagon
WSDP	W.S. DiPiero
DJD	D.J. Dutschke
DF	Dino Fabris
RF	Ruth Feldman
CF	Rina (Caterina) Ferrarelli
JG	Jonathan Galassi
MGT	Marisa Gatti-Taylor
KJ	Katherine Jason
FJ	Frank Judge
RL	Richard Lansing
DL	Donald Lourie
CM	Charles Matz
RAM	RoseAnna Mueller
RM	Richard Milazzo
AN	Art Neisberg
IN	Ida Nolemi
JP	Jan Pallister
EP	Edgar Pauk
JP	John Pellerzi
SR	Sonia Raiziss
MR	Martin Robbins
LS	Lawrence R. Smith
BS	Brian Swann
LV	Lawrence Venuti
JY	John Yau

ITALIAN POETRY TODAY

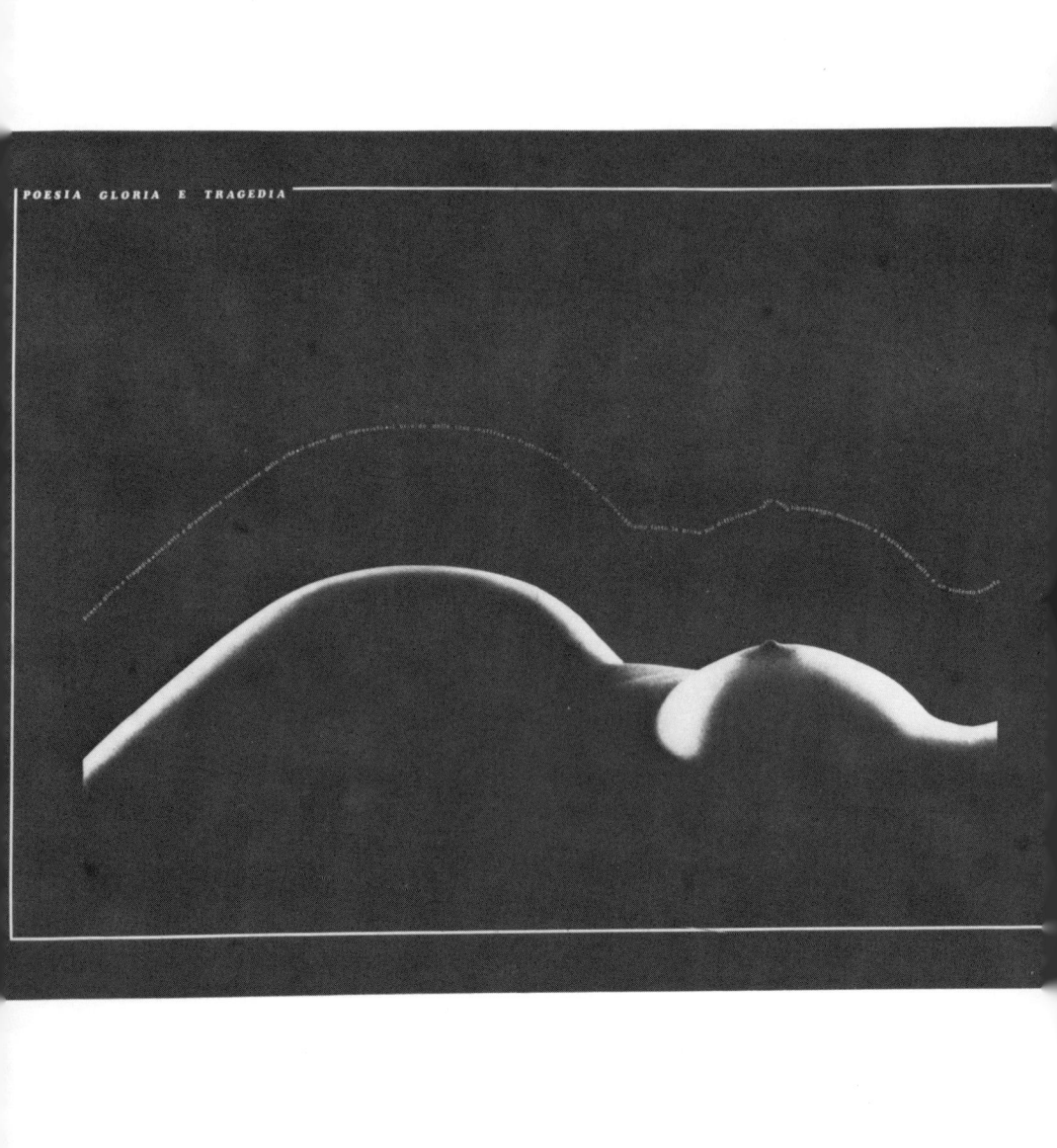

POESIA GLORIA E TRAGEDIA

Nanni Balestrini

THE INSTINCT FOR PRESERVATION

The story's about (can a fish live
long on dry sand? sleep without
a pillow?) man's life is all
an attempt (I don't have the slightest
idea, I've never felt sadder):

nevertheless once he disguised himself
as a milkman, on the other hand (I
looked for a more comfortable position
on the chair) it cannot live long
(we spent the rest of the night
seated, wracked by hunger,
waiting for daybreak).

Then he went up to the topmost
floor, like the highest trees
in the snow (describe the places
around you, if possible)
and the clock hand seemed to turn
too slowly; no one saw him,
everybody's sleeping.

(The same sensation, so, remain
seated, doubt it; let us unbutton
more weeks, and still the wound,
the sniffles, open hands that soil
the water, as long as they haven't
followed us. The wound, red like a horse).

The fever high like the snow, only
one button he thought. An enormous
saving of time. A cavil—yes? it gallops
(let's talk about it, the character
deserves remembering). He went up
to the very top.

The thin metal sheeting pierced (could
I have something to drink?) in the clip-
ings of time (he doesn't answer) snatches
branches from the woods (a fish bone against
his palate) on a sled loaded with snow
(he's disappeared) sprung from no one

knows where (and small bones all over
the floor) and hail on the meadow
sprouting on the painted landscape;
in the shape of a water-drop tallest
towering bell-ringer, lying in the bottom
of the tower, drinking in great gulps.

(CF)

from BODIES IN MOTION AND BODIES IN BALANCE

I

We could have done without them
trees are too noisy, but
what good are horses,
each on his own would have
managed to get lost,
to come back, to do
anything you want, some-
times trees succeed
in growing towards the sky
inhaling the explosion
of the unexpected moment, waiting
for the rain to stop, inspired
by instinct running from side
to side briskly, incited by hysteria

their heart full of buttons,
submerged eel-like fingers
so beautiful from the boat,
let's blow on it, the end.

VII

Sooner or later the tendon
is broken, the cut phalanx
chases the wind in the cage

and always the same obstinate
bird, the air to be inhaled through
the mouth full of blood

and on the swallowtailed body
crumpling minute by minute
a summer, filamentous, and the lichens

encrusted, enmeshed, the contractions
everytime you cough
now yellow now green now never

lost dangling from the hook
the sharks that surface, graze
the flesh by dint of saying it,

but in fact, who's ever seen them,
the horses? the summer was hot,
the crowd walked slowly.

(CF)

Luigi Ballerini

ENGLONDE OR THEREABOUTS

1

The operation consists
of pressing hard against the cavity
walls keeping the formula
in mind
      in case of apathy
the serum falls on the throat's
bitter jewels
          even a tourist sees
this hermaphrodite's a copy

2

the report is cleaned up
love in the way the journey reasserts
the hydra and look out for:
            itinerant calendars enwrap
            legless dogs
            the will of acids is fear

on the gums pleasure
in the indictment species
in the hybrid when
we pull together the accounts the wine-press
will be a prison

3

for this debt my sterling's valid
investiture and transoceanic
            spaces
ignis fatuus on graves around
memory
      the invention

of labyrinths measures
the blood of prophecy

      4

the century was not born
from indicted ashes by double
mandate the door was ajar
      and after her death
drifting over the river
she said she had enjoyed
      her forty-year reign
even if London wasn't a paradise
appointments had to be made
      to knights errant
to avoid further corruption
of the social fabric
in an age already crisis-ridden

      (1972)

      (RF & BS)

fragments from ONOMAREMALOGUS

one as if desert and beset
umbra
    (from Mars)
           versus
ira
  (one of the two horses)
two as if curtain

       *

      is double if circular
               if it renounces
     genitive
        (the divided does not coincide)
                       eros
    (askant to go under)
             is margin of the double
   *

memory is latitant memory
(from species to genus
set in seige, I-we besiege)

      *

    if it ensues itself
    its memory is isosceles
    if it precedes
    (before the prior)
    compatible with white

    black of absences invades the sound

                      (RM)

Dario Bellezza

WHAT SEX IS DEATH?

What sex will you be when I encounter you,
if hotheaded Orpheus doesn't look at me
and Eurydice was a lazy sow?

Farewell my folly gulped down
hastily in a thicket,
the flavor is lost in the night of delinquents
who blackmail their progeny with the slaps
of certainty, in suburban movie houses.

But what sex is death?
It's a boy. A girl. Frighteningly maternal
it embraces me on the threshold of sleep,
when dawn speeds up its agony,
and day heightens its melancholy colors;
and the sex begs its erections not to do
too much harm, not to overexcite
the silent companion of the night;
the watchful bosom stays then to listen
to my need of prayer recited out loud:
"Lord, unharmed I await judgment, await my death.
I await it only as executioner, devil's
advocate, in a Celimontano Papal Court office.

Sink me in sure earth. That I need not,
in death, suffer my survival.

Lord, make me die utterly and forever.
Let the dead not have me as their dead companion.
The day of my creation is far off,
the day of my destruction near at hand."

(RF)

[Untitled]

If war comes
I won't go as a soldier.

But once again worn-out trains
will carry young soldiers off
to die far from their mothers.

If war comes
I won't go as a soldier.

I'll be a betrayer
of my futile country.

I'll get myself shot
as a deserter.

        When I was small, my grandma
        used to tell me:
        "You weren't born yet; your mother
        was expecting you. In the shelter,
        obscene but warm with all those bodies,
        squeezed tightly against one another,
        seeming like so many brothers,
        I was already thinking of the stories
        that would put you to sleep, you
        who would, please God,
        see no more wars."

(RF)

[Untitled]

Your grandmother so like mine, innocent
creature who succeeded splendidly at becoming
a grandmother, used to live with your mother in a modest
but cheerful and happy house where you didn't find
the imaginary space for raids into the world
which from year to year changes mores and customs
for restless psychedelic youth
no longer drugged with wine and politics, like
mine, but already — at fifteen, sixteen — with sex and heroin,
and it's fortune's wish that the roads
of life reunite us for the moment
in that luminous house where your grandmother, like mine,
dying, said goodbye sadly to sons and nephews
shortly after the light meal to which I'd been invited
looking forward to a nice cake, having nibbled
several slices. All grandmothers resemble one another, perhaps,
I don't know much about the universe
of grandmothers, but if they're grandmothers through and through,
with the tale of Little Red Riding Hood brightening
our earthly childhoods, before trespassing
in colleges or streets starved for drugs or demonstrations
against fascism, the resurgent kind, the new
fascism that smears walls with nazi slogans
of violence or blows up trains in tunnels.
If they are dyed-in-the-wool grandmothers, they get thanked,
while you're eating a slice of cake, even if you were
too young to understand that, gobbling it down,
I was obeying a little imp of memory, finding
my sweet old grandmother again. We went home
in the mood to exchange confidences; and I told you the depressing
story of my grandmother's end, alone, living out her days
in the anguish of having been abandoned by everyone; remorse
still visits me at night in dreams and wakes me
to punishment no expiation can wipe out
beyond the despicable hell of the imagination.

(RF & BS)

Piero Bigongiari

from **MOSES**

He sinks in dryness,
iridescent locust-shell,
who risked drowning in a cradle,
but a woman comes forward: the outstretched hands
that saved you are not hers,
hidden object floating with the current
of the broad stream, that Nile
which flows in everyone's thoughts.
To say hands is to call them spread in a fan,
is to call them the sea, hidden object, yet
hidden subject on the horizon or in the breast.

And suddenly she said:
                    If the well-water
is no longer yours or mine, the water in the hand's hollow
is all but mine, drenched drop
the hand carries to your trembling thirst
trampled beside the well by his restless camels.

A quiet man, tent-dweller,
lodged in your breast, you say to Sarah
with the voice that God used
amid the rumbling of carts: you say it
in this shuffling of thirsty ones,
shepherds or animals: your tent
pitched in the desert like a moon
damp with heaven's warnings.

The one with pierced hands, perhaps
his own blood did it: reverse stigma,
the piercing comes from the ground,
from the trees the meadow the desert
slippery with locust-shells where the foot
sinks as if on crackling glass,
from the thick of humanity to which you offer yourself, Zipporah,
while you open your hands toward heaven.

                                                (RL)

MEMBRANE

The pink sheepskin that has carried the Gospels of Sinop
from what penury it nurtures the golden initials praising the Lord,
wrinkled wasteland from which the words are born.
It lacked only this absurd color of the setting sun
for the long desperate shudder that the sheep-word suffered
beneath the sun's gold raining down on the long-drawn-out death.
And now here it is a desert seeded with signs
that signify, that teach only their own origins,
bestial burden, ancient rape, being everywhere here,
fragile golden rain in the dryness of a sheepskin.

(RL)

Alfredo Bonazzi

WHO KNOWS WHERE IT'S WRITTEN

So, sitting like an old man,
I was filling my loneliness
with ants.
I'd even sleep during the day
to increase my detachment
from the boy knocked
into the pit of slime.
No, you weren't there then, dearest,
when I'd pull myself up with effort
and drag my body
from window to gate
from gate to window.

My only means of surviving
springtimes in prison
was to ignore the weariness of the night
and hold back the stars on the sea.
Winter's end: new sap
stirred things and my heart.
I saw the earth prepare
to fill the empty spaces
and stretch branches to the plants.
Until evening,
amid glimmers of still cold sun,
I'd hear a childish gutter laugh
and — getting sharper —
the blue scream
at the tangle of bars.

Who knows where it's written
that the chrysalis is a butterfly
destined for the hidden perfume
of a flower among stones
and that only love

can turn psalms of grief
into Gregorian chants.
Being in prison doesn't matter. Life
has reached me just the same;
it has the gift of your voice
and the infinite hope
of new buds on the willow.

Now I'm alive, dearest —
don't ask me how.

(FJ)

TWENTY THOUSAND YEARS OF WAITING

There's twenty thousand years of waiting
in this place
the stones
set up strawmen
that don't defend the grain from sparrows
or ants from the jailer's step

Stone slabs don't pick up prints;
only hands rest on iron gratings.
An old gull scans
the surface of the sea.

And an eclipse projects the forbidden WOMAN.

On the climbing shadows
of evening
the twenty thousand years of stone are yawning.

(FJ)

I DON'T HARVEST THE WIND

I don't harvest the wind
when the night carries salt
and hares chased by hounds,
shimmers of light
and red fruits hanging
on the point of seed:
the dwarf foliage of the lindens lengthens
and owl eyes appear in the sky.

I don't harvest the wind
when it creates other nights in the night
coupling skeletons
in an obscenity of death.
A wire becomes an arc
a sheet a sail
an acorn a bullet
and a thought a love.

I don't harvest the wind
when it splits the cross of branches at night
and plays a melody on blades of grass
for hidden crickets,
while an owl sways
on a swinging branch.

When I have moon arms
on your heart of yellow daisies.

(FJ)

FAIR COPY NOTEBOOK

Tonight, downstairs,
a boy dressed as an old man
slit the veins of his neck.
In his shrunken hand a razor,
and a cardboard smile
wrung from his chest.
On the fair copy notebook
a weary farewell
and an enclosed request
to be taken back home.

When your hair
makes a barrier for your face
to hide your eyes from me,
before forgetting
the sun dissolved on my lips,
I feel like a hermit
guarding painful silences.
I'd be a distracted thing,
forgotten like a useless object;
for a heart I'd have a blind alley,
and the memory of the dead for memories.

Careful, my son,
because the myths are dead ...
They've taken the heart
from that white-bearded boy
and haven't sent him home.

(FJ)

Edith Bruck

BIRTH

Feeling the urge my mother
made for the privy at the far end of the courtyard
and strained strained with all her might
plagued by her painful constipation.
"It's like giving birth", she kept saying to herself
and strained strained harder
broad forehead dripping sweat
bluegreen eyes full of tears
veins swollen on the white neck
untouched by real or imitation jewels.
The kerchief slipped off
showing her dark hair;
with both hands she held onto the swollen belly with me inside.
To readjust her head-covering
like a good Orthodox Jewess she let go of her belly
and kept straining straining.
The next thing was a cry   a long-drawn-out wail:
my head almost grazed the pit full of excrement.
A busy neighbor woman
ran to her aid and that's how I was born.
According to the gypsies a lucky future was in store for me;
for my father I was another mouth to feed
for my mother an unavoidable calamity
that befalls poor religious couples who make love
as a gesture of peace after months of quarrels
for my five not seven brothers
(luckily two died young)
a real toy that squealed
sucked at the wrinkled nipples
clung to the skin of mama's empty breasts
a mother undernourished like the mothers
of Asia Africa India South
or North America of yesterday today tomorrow . . .

(RF & BS)

SISTER ZAHAVA

Sister Zahava in the language of the Bible
your name means gold
gold like your adolescent heart
in a volcanic body
with two mature eyes of black flame
a fiery mouth
that spat words of love for your little sister
in the enemy's face
with your arms of rock
that sprang up in my defense from a sea
of melted lead to push me to survival
rich with our renewed hopes
with insane stubborness
in the struggle for an existence
its fabric already turning necrotic
and the threads which memory's hook
fished up again more and more rotted
fell to pieces remembering
a childhood full of humiliations
insults at school jeers in the street
misery at home under a straw roof
that dripped rain and my uncle smelling of wine
his fat hands joined in prayer
between my pure legs
a life
lived beside walls
abandoned even by the dogs
taught to piss up against
living or murdered Jews
behind the barbed wire
where the only living thing was death.
Then—the Liberation!
Afterwards a new beginning
it seemed the fabric held
the thin thread was transformed
to rope for a definitive mooring
I was ready finally
for the burst of gratitude

mutual salvation
when the rope broke
and here I am far from you alone
on the bank of the nothingness that has caught me up
beyond the limits of suffering
today hangs suspended
no longer asks anything
doesn't wish for life or death:
the light of your gold heart
offered from beyond the Ocean
gutters out in my darkness.

(RF & BS)

Ferdinando Camon

TO THE UNKNOWN SOLDIER

To the lady teacher looking for material
for a lesson on the homeland, a soldier
sent an envelope of crab-lice from the front,
captured from his own groin hair.
The bugs got crushed in transit.
The little teacher pointed her finger
at the red stains, saying: a wounded soldier
has sent me some of his very own blood.

(MR)

HE COULD HAVE

He could have
taught us something
our father, not just sat there
staring at the crusted fog

that penetrates the skin
of tart apples, sucked
later by a stray rabbit,
not us.

He could have sat us on his bike
and given us a ride to school,
the streets we walked in solitude
are heavy under our feet.

When snowy days
beseiged us in our shanty

he could have responded to our
quick glances.

He could have
talked to us
slapping our necks
instead of keeping silent,
taking it out on his oxen,
patting their rumps.

He could have
caressed us,
made us
a rag doll
not checked the yoke each day
so the ox wouldn't suffer.

At the table he could teach us
right from wrong
but there's not much meat
and no salt.

                                            (MR)

Giorgio Caproni

LARGHETTO

    Outside the barrier, perhaps.
Perhaps, beyond the Customshouse
of Water . . .

    Where the canal
already runs to grass, and the wind
already smells of the country . . .

                    Try.

    Childhood is there.

              Try.

    Trembling childhood is there . . .

    There, still, the man
with a mutilated arm, with the left
(remember: you were *ordered*)
— scarcely a child, then,
who smiles at tigers)
fires the pistol
at the sheet of paper held up to it . . .

                    You go away . . .

    Try where the flocks
are clouds on the meadow . . .

    The old man with his dark
eyes . . .

        It may be him.

    Try where fear

splits even the sky, and breath
(remember; you were *ordered*)
trembles like the wool
of hedges . . .

        Outside

the barrier . . .
          Beyond
the Customshouse of Water . . .

                Where
— without oak-grove and without
tent — I,
in the aluminum rainbows
of the three, did not recognize
any God of extermination.

    Try.

       Beyond evil
and good.

       Where
the wind already smells of steel,
and the canal is a knife.

                 (RF)

Giovanni Cecchetti

NEW YEAR'S MORNING IN PASADENA

I

Bundles of birds erupt
                radiant, from the South

and bears seesaw
with stags feeding on clumps of sage.
Don't grieve if they don't know today
is the first of the year. If you dive
into the mallow you'll escape
                the rebuke of the past.

Tomorrow the Colorado will rise, a swirling pool,
to cancel even the stars
when the trees that cannot walk now
will be as they were the day of their birth
                But now a plane fords by,

great banana-fish,

                sleek joy
over the melting gulf air, until it scrapes
against the rainbow spattering you with jade.

II

If television brings you
parade floats of butterfly roses, time's
cloak is shortened and you stand
on the cliffs of day, your hands
clipping singed clots, still
locked in yesterday. You seek a lightning flash
of eternity, but reap
not even a glimmer flung from its edge.

It's only the first of the year. Suspend
the gray solfeggio of the autumns
squeezed with caged breath
from the non-thawing earth and the overhanging
falcon wave. Yes,
that hour too will come. Not today,
when bundles of butterfly angels move
soft friendly wings to Pasadena.

(DJD)

TOWARDS MONTREAL

I

From forty thousand feet the earth
is patchwork carpet in relief – Mont Blanc
coeval to the Rockies, and your eyes
never tiring
of snowy masts in hairless hollows.

This is today's orbit, nailed
to the window, jammed into turbine
air, inside a box floating
in the wind and the stunned hum
of the engines – dazed men and women
tearing up a hem of globe.

Impossible to land. Impossible to
embrace the snow or dip our feet
in the rhythm of hollows.

II

Clipped prairies corrode the journey
of the Saint Lawrence, gushing ships along
and dreaming great cascades of flamingos
blooming on layers of ice —
with mole men forever vanished.

But ghosts of birches walk
white in the wind. The earth
forgets the panting of summer,
here where the engines have seized time
and shaken off the hours — dead
fringes of November. Impossible to land.

This is the orbit of always, wedged
into the seat's prison. If you make a move
it grips you fast, grimacing;
and yet it dives into neither an end
                nor a beginning.

                              (DJD)

Guido Ceronetti

THE APOCALYPSE

The Lamb broke seal Number One
And out of the book came a sleek white horse
A man rides it armed with a bow
He wins the joust and takes the crown
The day was lovely and the morning clear
The earth will fall into total ruin

Seal Number Two was shattered
And out came War on a red horse
They gave the knight a sword
To wreak great slaughter
The day was lovely and the morning clear
The earth will fall into total ruin

When seal Number Three was split
Witness the black horse of Hunger
The knight sets all the grain aflame
And leaves the wine and oil for tomorrow
The day was lovely and the morning clear
The earth will fall into total ruin

At the tearing of seal Number Four
I saw Death on a yellow horse
With Hell close by her on the croup
Sowing wounds gallows and other knives
The day was lovely and the morning clear
The earth will fall into total ruin

The Lamb also broke seal Number Five
Under an altar the unavenged shades
Of the prophets who were killed
Show their blood so it may be paid for
The day was lovely and the morning clear
The earth will fall into total ruin

When Number Six was breached
Quaking earth and sun gone black
Blood moon and rain of broken stars
All of us plunged deep within the mountains
The day was lovely and the morning clear
The earth will fall into total ruin

Dead silence at the Seventh seal
Amid loud thunder an angel throws down
The rose of a flaming censer
And the whole world is a fiery silence
The day was lovely and the morning clear
The earth will fall into total ruin

An alcoholic star fragments
Reclining drunkenly on the waters
He who drinks it dies of a burnt throat
Dark fell and the light grew quiet
The day was lovely and the morning clear
The earth will fall into total ruin

You have heard what was revealed to John
On the Isle of Patmos
When you have swallowed every evil
You will see the good for a thousand years
The day was lovely and the morning clear
The earth will fall into total ruin

(RL)

Giorgio Chiesura

THE HOUSES OF THE GERMANS

Lisdero came back in the morning
with something delicate in his hands
and a special smile on his hollowed-out
face; he was holding a violet he'd picked
near the barbed wire during
"his breath of fresh air"
(that breath of fresh air he takes in
every morning with his skinny pale
scholar's chest, figuring out aloud
the "advantages" this will bring
to his health, but in reality
just feeling and enjoying the liquid
beauty of those first fresh breaths
in solitude).
It had been pulled up with minute attention
with all its thin roots, and planted
with care in a condensed milk can
in the sand he'd brought in his pocket,
then placed on the windowsill.
And it was such a prisoner's gesture,
such a classic from *Le mie prigioni*
that we all laughed watching him.
But he wanted to explain it to us;
he did not speak of nature or spring
of longing for sunshine or Italy or other,
he only said with that quick laugh of his:
"Here it is. This way the entire
community can enjoy it."
Then he added: "It will remind
us a little of the houses of the Germans
that always have so many flowers at the windows..."

Everyone was quiet, astonished,
because no one had expected to hear this.

(CF)

PATRIOTIC HYMNS

Today twenty or thirty Russians
gathered near the barbed wire fence
and started singing songs to us
as a sign of friendship.
Immediately a group formed spontaneously
in our camp to answer with more songs.

The Russian ones were strong and deep
military and folk-songs,
march rhythms full of melancholy
as of marches on steppes and plains
and they sang like believers, absorbed.
I felt our inferiority:
by comparison ours seemed
silly and stupid.
I also thought that the Russians
had already sung theirs in the past
marching and fighting for their country,
while the ones with which we answered
were country rounds or popular songs:
we've had to repudiate
all our patriotic *hymns*.

But all the same I felt it a duty
to stay and sing for the Russians
because even country rounds and popular songs
were signs of friendship toward them.
And I stayed to sing till the end,
even when the heavy rain started
until the Germans let loose their dogs
and on both sides we fled saying goodbye.

(CF)

THE PARLOR

The Jewish girls from Poland who courteously invite us
to have tea with them and who have made
a kind of parlor here in the attic,
are a small group who live apart
from the others and stay here with the Italians.
They are young and each one of them
has a number tattooed on her arm.
They have been in the *lager*
since they were children.
They are the only survivors of entire
families dead in camps and burned.
And I do not understand where they could
have learned their parlor manners and their lady-like
ways, and even less why they want to do this
and why it means so much to them, they're so
stubborn, here where everything is free
and unbridled, and truer for every one
after so much suffering, and where they could
have found those rags of shawls and those cushions.

(CF)

Pietro Cimatti

*On a bench at San Lorenzo Outside the
Walls, a summer morning. Singe, limier
de femmes . . . ou même, au besoin, femme
(Corbière)*

A white-haired friar walks
on the asphalt on swift sandals,
a sanctuary of robe, swords, crosses
indifferent airy over us the weary.

The world's for us—it's for me—
                      the fall
from paradise of infancy to nothing:
for him a climbing with burning
                            forehead
through the unlived life.

I know the terror and black desires in him:
he's the richest and the poorest,
                    the most handsome
and the monster, old child, young bull
sacrificed *ad gloriam sacri imperii.*

Lava eyes, he goes to eat
                christ
goes to share him with toothless old women,
dark mansion, rope, boiling oils,
crusader of contempt, whip. Sad.

                                    (FJ)

NOVEMBER

To Raoul

November: I must go to the cemetery.
Chrysanthemums are expensive; I take
two carnations — they'll do. My grief
would be more sincere with a train
of white flowers, a cemetery so full
you'd get dizzy. But they'll do. The dead
don't see, don't smell —
I could even bring a sheathless flask,
a worn-out ladle, a basketful
of old tram tickets: what do
the dead care what you bring?
They don't look at your hands, they don't know.
More dead each year, further away,
they don't even know tomorrow is
their birthday: November 2nd.
Forgetful, they're empty-headed.

In a hundred years everything I love
will be nothing. From this yellow house
I see endless funerals leave:
sextons descend from every floor,
load up and leave. From the gardens
comes the fog: I grow old: youth
died with the man who died — whoever has
a birthday tomorrow, forever. Two carnations
will do.

(FJ)

from I WALK ALONG THE WALLS AND HAVE LOST MY SHADOW

They're beautiful, the lopped heads, a clean job.
Even more beautiful the bloodless legs,
color of sugar-coated almonds.
I have loved the hair lost on dunes;
I collect scattered pubes and arm-pits
of no woman.
With years of servitude and patience I pay
homage to an odd buttock, proof of endurance.
I want to shut myself up with a head neck
torso two stumps two wrists
two tibias two shin-bones a medulla
two feet two hands, etc. (in a safe
place underground and never be found again)
everything totally falling to pieces,
crammed like must into a suitcase and hidden
in a safe place, jammed tight,
and never be disturbed.
They're beautiful those holes dug in the woods
then filled in and stamped down,
                                      and that's all.

                                            (RF)

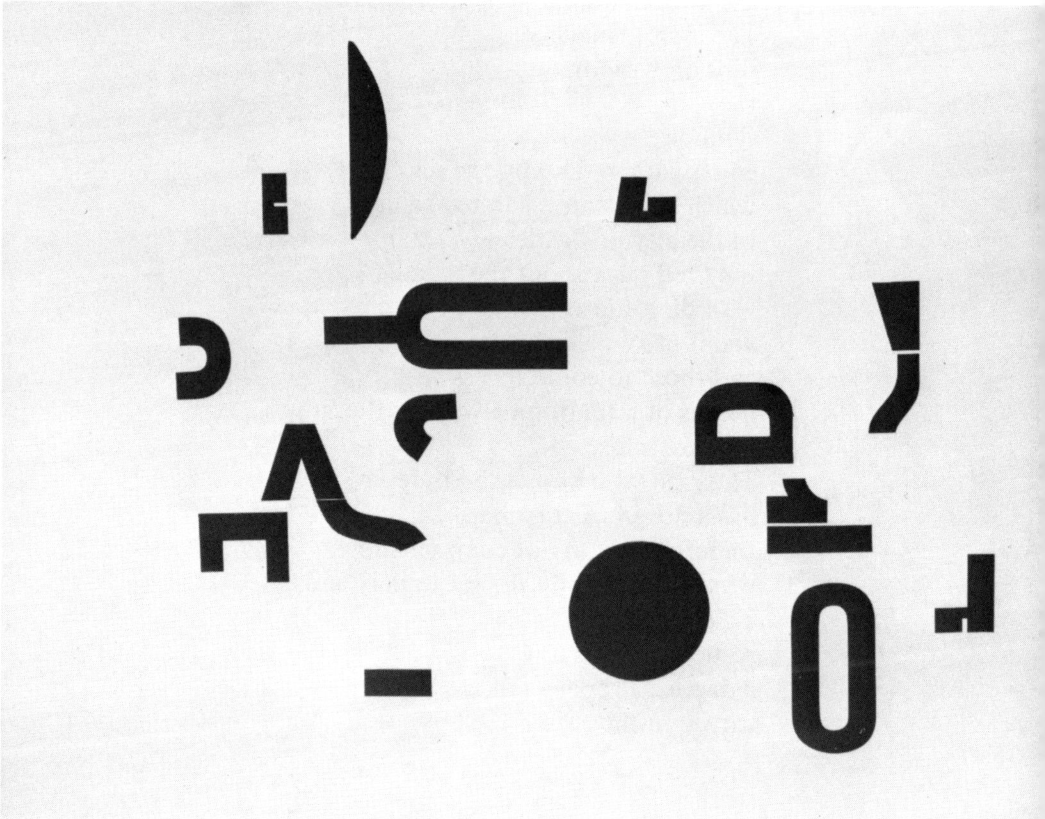

Elena Clementelli

from ETRUSCAN NOTEBOOK

1

Cerveteri road:
over the drowsy voice of the pines
the long death contains stone words.
The secret language
slips on weapons,
tools,
symbols,
and is gathered up by the sea
which alone can speak to the dead.
In the city of the dead
they tell tales about the living,
with discretion:
about us
and those to come,
heroes of a tradition always in the future
timeless gods.
The man who has bested time
has a different grammar,
therefore we do not comprehend
what the sea, only the sea understands.
To distract
restless curious boys,
a dagger, a rope, a fan,
carved in the tufa.

2

Not what you were,
the daily sign
repeated by air's mirror
which the mistral pushes
beyond thresholds of secret mourning.
The projection of the days

peopled with gestures
contradicts death's lazy will.
An immense breath
opens the tufa's pores,
stirs the sleep of cold couches
In the violated darkness
a presence rejects the legend
and a people of effigies
rises from the sea's soft silence
that restrains each voice and leads it back.
The embers glow,
the trumpets
sound the hunt, war,
household objects jingle.
Not what you were.
What you are. Alive.

6

And the Great Bear
bends the weight of the equinox
which the tired October moon
crushes onto the Etruscan hills,
last shield.
The silent season
warms the voices of the long evening
in the city of Tarchon.
The towers are antennae
of subterranean rites.

9

On the rough flight of the road
that runs to the sea
the quiet eye of Volterra opens.
Victorious day
after the false night
lowered like death's eyelid
to bar light.
Mad commands of war,

frantic work to raise
a hasty stone wall:
today a distant nightmare, a stone marker.
Free under the pure Etruscan sky
the tufa stretches to its architecture,
survivor of love in life.
Again the arch
that saluted other entrances in another peace
welcomes the familiar sound of human footsteps,
the stupor of the glance
under time's weight
that from earth's salty gray
grazes the enigma of the three faces,
weighs on the inert guarded memories.

The wind's voices are of happy dawns
in the motionless twilight
where the thin figure lengthens
—prodigy, projection, prophecy—
pain of evening's shadow
or endless echo of the sun?

(RF & BS)

Roberto Coppini

from THIRTEEN POEMS

I

The provisions arranged, they tied up the baggage carts
and the horses, the last arrivals jostling one another
in order to see better.

Let everyone born on this day be slain.

The stars are dying too. The house regurgitates
miasmas, the band of fog on spires and observatories.

V

See? I put a sign on your back, but the wound-inflictor
has drawn back his hand seventy-seven times with impunity.

A man does not talk for the end
of this or of another kingdom:
a man speaks in memory of himself.

The tree has stones instead of leaves
and fruit. The sea closes upon the drift
of the continents.

VII

The body which is searched in its folds
does not rebel. Everything has a purity of its own
less than the word this temptress to perjury and all
who furnishes the desert with small fortresses.

Pollen puffs up the eyes. I appear
behind the house, I question the bird's flight,
the intense toil of the ant, which stores
food for a winter yet to come.

IX

A name is neither a relic nor a Siamese
twin born dead
from whom it's impossible to detach oneself.

The night of ashes the head
rolled away by itself. Beyond every
possible happening, I fear

a second birth, the forced
migration from one point to another
of my body. I arrange myself

in an empty river bed. The friend
who you think is sleeping has been dead
for three days.

X

From here one feels nothing. Somewhere
or other I forgot my bloodstained
shoe, but an imprint

follows me everywhere. Because a fratricide
had already been seen, but no one had ever seen
the killing of a dead man. The tents of the merchants
—cheats, counterfeiters, slave-vendors —
sink in the slime. There are those who cannot
draw near the table for fear of the dogs.

Hunger, not manna: painless
rain, scattered to the four winds.

XIII

We might not have been born. The crow
and the dove vanish in the void.
If a man — or his enemy — surfaces
from the waves, I throw the rope
to both.

(JP & AN)

Raffaele Crovi

EYES

This light that filters from the wall
that closes the tunnel
through the screen of air
my breath opposes to the void
does not interrupt fear.
When a cat meets another cat at night
its fur stands up on end and it trembles:
its eyes printed on the dark
record the prodigy of other eyes
that see ghosts.
Better to be blind than glimpse
the flash of the match that primes
the fuse that makes the earth explode.

(RF)

FLORA

The leaf loses water, grows scaly,
seems the skin of a baby polluted
by radium: it curls up
along the veinings and, bent,
offers no screen to the flower, which unfolds
and drops as though lopped by a blade.

(RF)

IN THE BUNKER

The pine is splintered
where lightning struck; lichen
that grows there turns to white mould.
In the snow-reservoir, full of water,
a toad stirs, chews waterlilies.
Light, however, infiltrates the house
violating every room with Bach.
In the walnut *trumeaux* papers, not mice,
make nests: life has blunted
the smooth inlays of objects.
From the mantelpiece the lacquered *marschallin*
strikes quarters and hours:
the snaky handle pretends to affirm
that time is eternal and consumes us;
but this is no museum, it's our bunker.
Dust doesn't corrode bronze or enamel:
by using we preserve, knowing
that we're transforming an orderly paradise
into a purgatory of utensils.

(RF)

Maurizio Cucchi

GETTING UP ON THE WRONG SIDE OF THE BED

1

Winding the alarm-clock until you almost
break the spring. (All alone
in the dark of night during the August holidays.) Prepared
to be present at the ritual film-nightmare. The dominant
theme stands out
in the lens's panting pursuit
and in its progressive sadistic drawing away.

Among other things: "dreamed of so-and-so —
but who was it? he too dead of cancer
in the space of two days." And continuing
— incidentally — "downright
haunted by the ludicrous fear of getting
out of bed very very quietly
and knifing her at night while walking in my sleep."

2

Going back to base: appointment blackmail start-
ing out. The tram's delay. Sudden
breakdowns. Unknown parts of the city
terror a knot in your stomach strange streets. Greyish
suburbs. Steady anguished sensation of being more and more behind
schedule. But
let's look each other right in the eye. At this point
without making a thing about it or at the very most
pretending it's nothing. My pulse my pulse
taking my pulse is the least
I can do. Auscultate
auscultate — that's what's needed. The neck. Twisting
forward and backward. But all useless. The heart
is unreachable. But a failure a crick
a crack a small hole a micro-

cog a tic
a tiny bone a fingernail an eyeball
a small gland.

3

A quarter to five. The hour strikes. The hand
dangling on the night-table. (But already before,
looking every half-hour
at the clock seeing with suspicion
so as to press observe
know verify. Darkness and cold in the house
hollow languor in the stomach. A few
habitual actions (for ex.: mirror, soap, water,
coffee with milk, clothes, suitcases, lock). And
outside to the cold No. 91 bus stop.

Going back again to base: But
the flight might be considered checked. In spite of
shots chase anxiety
accomplice irreparable
irremovable accusations.
(Proceeding with a hypothesis of homicide
keeping your eyes peeled for a while).

4

A certain heaviness in the legs
(stemming from overwhelming fatigue or
out-of-hours amorous activity)
bestows on me a sufficiently afflicted look. So that
I too share other people's problems, in some ways,
opportunely passing over them.   At the door
a clever young man dressed in black
was performing exorcisms.   But in reality
things went very differently:

5

regular arrival of the bus. Manoeuvre
clearing, rural church, bells mass embrace
kiss happiness. Stop. But what became of appointment chase
flight shots lynching, of the missed
arrival of the tram, of the errors enroute:

"But nothing my dear finally
a bit of relaxation for us too"

: "and Sunday evenings
                 when we're there nice and quiet
                       we eat outdoors."

6

So, like a bolt from the blue the telex blow:
"HE DIED SUDDENLY. HE WAS LOSING BLOOD
FROM THE MOUTH AND FROM THE EARS."

                                              (RF)

THE TREASURE MAP

It all started a few days ago.
The woman concierge reported to me that she saw him go out
very quietly in the early afternoon. (Jacket from the
       clothes-rack, "I'll be right back". He disappears.) And I say
the nastiest people swear he doesn't give a damn
about his mother, his young brother;   some swear that "he phones
from time to time puts in an appearance, suave, smiling";
others insist they've seen him
wandering through the Public Gardens
between a tree, a pedal-car,
a child's bike,

remembering, mumbling, resting
on a granite bench. Drinking a coffee, something.

(random clues, drawn bodily from impressions, if I were
    he
in person)

(a sound of footsteps, seeing her pass in the hall; temptation
    on the tip of one's tongue, or silent. Oaths
    shameful
insults.   An anguish, in the leisure hours of a smart
well-mannered little boy.
                      Irresistibly
later everything told to the priest at confession. To her,
even).

(late in the evening. Along in a corner, on the ground, knees
    black.
Disappeared into bed who knows how

                                    "but what am I doing here?
what happened?" Quickly under the covers. But then the light
still on, in the room, beyond; the candy
that won't melt in the mouth. Getting up, knocking, "may
    I", putting it
on the night-table. Only then to sleep).

Later on staring at the window-panes; making yourself be tossed
about by the passersby; standing still in a meadow.

2

you see him return with the "CORRIERE", relaxed;
saying things like "how much less, travelling
by streetcar or subway
can one listen to what people are saying. Reading
the pages of other people's books, sharing
their problems. Contemplating,
unseen, details of faces, clothes."
                          Smiling

in search of the alarm clock: "I don't have to get up
early in the morning — or late. All the same, every evening
I set the alarm. At 8
(or 9). I hear it ring and I stay put. I sleep,
laze. Maybe it's good for me."

Among the rumors collected a phrase
uttered, repeated, heard more or less by everybody:
"I saw...you know perfectly well...that cripple. Well,
he says he's going away, in search of something
out of the ordinary, who knows what. Business;
maybe he went mad."

(but the fact is, the concierge explained to me, eyes lifted to heaven,
"him, him? Anything but..."

3

Sure, it's probably, for the most part, foolish fantasies.
The fact is that he was following
a trail, inside or out,
a track,
a vague indication. With his clues,
again now his good information.

. . . .
. . . . . .

Before I stop, I recall, among his favorite phrases,
this one:
"when I'm old I'll have more patience.
I'll feed the pigeons."

(RF)

Brandolino Brandolini d'Adda

FROM A SEA HARBOR

Your breast   my temples
veils   walled doors in wartime   strong-box
all the lost keys sing the round cruise
the evening anchor
in corroded metal to fuse
is weighed from childbelief

Pearls of elision whirling tops
         in windy verdant valiant valleys
miscarried is in luxuriance or frailness
the concluded word

To conclude or to vanish deceives us
kissing I with, you with
the companionless moon
the solo signal light, with nothing nothing

                              (CM)

KITCHEN GARDEN

Culturefact   kitchen garden
in which to leave or I enter folk-leader with demon cats
harrow ikon   matrix Earth   nosegay beds

kitchen garden   desire for seasoning
tail-docker in the habitat of extreme complexity
that plots against the gardener (Encyclopedia Treccani)

the descant from the fig tree to defoliant
thorngate deviates the pot-bellied desks

    stone cracks
    corymbose limbo
    delicate potatoes
unravel in such assured perimeter seeds from consuming and the
opening from the invasion. The weight of footsteps in the batter
for birth, the climber's grip into the beamhead, the bough necked
gardener floats the plot in chrysanthemum yellow swelling smoke,
fly away   fly away

garden graced
enflowering desire
Mary mine
lilywhite heart   heartened by deceit
in the external state
air glory morning glory
with legs stretched below   the horror of the selection if
the potherbs were to die to unrepresent
the thief of family trees, folk, embrix, flints. The trumpeter
trains and the curious winter cuckoo gathered up the noble serpent
that draws in century-long coils

I tie   untie
that dove from its vicious circuit
today there is something friendly under the sun
able   edible   seedable
a soldier's spade godmother is it
a planting of soulless
attributes well-nourished: essences extant.

Pathways first steps turned stones
genetics of watery
fruitcenter, all round out-culture

                                                              (CM)

Milo De Angelis

METAPHORS

The same low sky
of ambulances and rain, in the excitement,
and hands on the groin, summoned by the body
to oppose
the slightest numbness to things
while outside, among the traffic lights, Europe
which has invented the finite
resists
far from the beast, defends
real and irrelevant concepts
along the highways, in linear time toward a point:
the eyes don't close before things,
always true and then false,
where today a millenium wavered
between yielding and not yielding
losing itself always later, with intelligence.

(LV)

A LOSER

Outside is history
the struggling classes.
What can you do once and for all
rejecting the world
accepting it in the morning
("It was true, you know, the quarrel with her
was serious. But there was only one bed
in the shabby room
and bodies prevailed.

You need two beds and money to quarrel.")
There were biological
limits and great laws of profit:
everything was untouchable.
So gods and the interior were invented.
At night, during his erection
he even laid claim to fate
("where've you been
all my life?")

(LV)

FIRST COMES

"Oh if you knew:
whoever suffers
whoever suffers isn't serious."
Suburbs of Turin. Summer. By now
there isn't much water in the river, the news-stand is closed.
"Change, don't wait any longer."
There are only a few cars near the wall.
No one goes by. We sit for a while
on the parapet. "Maybe you can still
become unique, can
still feel without paying, can enter
into a depth that's not
commemorative: don't wait for anyone,
don't wait for me, if I suffer, not even for me."
And we stare at the dark water; a slight breeze
stirring it
gives it thin veins, like wood.
It touches my face.
"When will you break away, when will you have no
alternatives? Don't cling, accept
accept
losing something."

(LV)

Alfredo De Palchi

[Untitled]

Tomorrow is another day   no sun   only
the sky comes closer
electric with air that . . I mustn't surrender
to greedy existence or get damaged
                              somebody
something will restore me to a better life
but there's no prospect: I took one road
for another where I meet people I don't understand
& who know nothing /
                    so-called joy
is like carrying a pack on my back / why
dread that road /
I'm a dog scratching at his fleas /
power of the heart is a woman's
topic / & remember
                    nobody
crossed me up but myself

                                        (SR)

[Untitled]

Me, ashamed? of this three-dimensional
life that shuttles me from chair
to wheel & back again
completing its absurdity day
after day always shorter
cursed with my disdain & darkening
in the slow work of demolition
                    — beyond all this

there's no shaft of light but an unbroken
passage of wandering men:
it's my luck to resist these vague
faces
      — there's no way out

I'm a chain of insidious origins
orders mechanisms fantasies
already charged with extinction
gruel of mud, tedious hush
laid on the coals of the still living —
I / witness of each morning's crescendo /
am nothing at evening but the simple
shock of two extremes

                                  (SR)

[Untitled]

How can anyone swallow the tale our
daily story
hardened to great gulps of
insult or crumbs of it — under each leaf an insect
war travels darkly & everywhere the struggle
for survival: of the mouse   rabbit
hunter hawk planing from the sky's
contagion
        of the butcher's boy lashing at his bull
with ferocious joy & howling — now for the kill —

this greed of violence, of power
                            in us all

                                  (SR)

[Untitled]

The meaning of what we expect
or of the unexpected — the world grins under the fist —
we
have opted for not weeping not helping
but looking away when a body collapses,
walking off with the same indifference
we feel for the animal knocked over by a car
or a shotgun — it's useless to cry what a pity, to pretend

each one is all for himself
& stays locked in

(SR)

Arnaldo Di Benedetto

GRAFFITI FROM MERANO

I've watched my overseas contemporaries
on the movie screen.
A crowd of boys at the doorway of the third
age (cf. Alfieri) terribly sad;
a bleak provincial town in the USA. These kids
in technicolor drive cars
like battered shoes. There we were,
talking about football or basketball
— in Theater Square, at the usual corner, one foot
up on the railing
— or at some pool in Liberty Street.

(The one who was reading Ungaretti & Cardarelli
kept his mouth shut or covered up carelessly).

"Andrew doesn't go to church anymore."
"Politics is shit."
Jazz in the big classroom one afternoon;
an old-timer expounding styles & schools,
ancient history from Ravel to Gershwin...
Out of America rock'n'roll, realcool,
the Elvis frenzy & voices on disks
crooning *Only You.*
Those who were going steady paired off & left
joining us later. Some shared confidences,
others suffered in silence.
In love! *Le dernier outrage.*

Christel the skater was cutting figures
every winter evening in yellow light.
The svelte shadow glided across the ice.
Beginners & champions
as nonchalantly as they could
passed close by, even spoke to her, each
locked inside his own private game?   To move onto

the ice for her, to get near her!
Anyone who kissed her in the dark — first kiss —
found an unsure mouth, a rigid body,
dense silence
for the whole evening.
What hellish flames had licked her?
— And then the idiotic racing after friends,
the rumor almost true,
a few secret regrets.

The guy reading Cardarelli or Ungaretti
went off sometimes. By train,
second class, not by plane.

(SR)

Dio è un essere perfettissimo come una VOLKSWAGEN che...

...va... ...e va... ...e va...

Luciano Erba

FAR BEYOND THE FROZEN SEAS

I know a city
the accredited guide was saying
in the small fiery circle of a bonfire
with a very long iron bridge
suspended over a working-class quarter
I remember some cafés before the bridge
big stores a small synthetic
or Soviet theatre, I'm old
and I'm not sure, a real city
of women with top-hats
or with hobnailed shoes
it's probably easier to enter from the road
they were saying on the bridge with a sigh
and a brief gesture at the houses underneath,
the rooms...
The scientists encamped on the gravel
listened in silence to the guide
but no one asked how many days on horseback
it would take to reach the city.
They began to walk up and down:
rooms longer than they were wide
hyacinths at the double windows
gardens with strawberries and lettuce
in the kitchen reflections of fire
at dusk, tiled floors... The mission
of the Royal Geographical Society
was overcome by sleep. Tiled floors
by now the guide was saying to the stars.

(RF)

THE THOUGHTLESS ONE

But when are they coming? and how?
and who sends them among us?
one day you find them nearby
with peaked caps
red scarves, hands
in their front pant-pockets
new companions in our silent
games, smiling companions
smaller than us, paler
tired by a short run, awkward
at wrestling, jumping, weightless.
I remember one who climbed with us
on an October morning up to Mt. Cavallo
his cheeks red because of heart-trouble
he smiled running to keep up with us.
And another, it could even have been the same man
from that way they had of walking and the deep blue sweaters
who followed me through vineyards to the valley's end
to trout-fish where the river
branches into clear channels.
We stayed in the water until evening
without his once asking me
if he could try his luck: then he vanished
down a path I could not find again.
And a third man, or the same one again,
from that large knot they make in their wool scarves,
and from the way he stood near me, silent,
in the yellow fields outside the city
in an imagined Africa
through a long, still day. And a fourth . . .

Vanished. Felled by pitiless fevers,
consumed by an unknown evil, far off, I don't know.
Nor do I know if they will return nor when, nor how
friends, days, the brightest season,
in life — lost through carelessness —
will return.

(RF & BS)

INCOMPATIBILITY

As long as Don Oldani
and the twenty-five explorers
chase one another over these lead slabs
I picture to myself the tribe of women
of the oldest center of the city.
Asleep on upper floors
in iron beds
how many are dreaming of my silk scarf?
I look at the grey-red Sunday
city, from the cathedral terrace
but if only I could fly
to the lovely geraniums on the long balconies
pass through doors, walk
barefoot on the red hexagons
then see myself in your mirrors
dark girls, who live in the garden!
Now the crusaders leave
I stay up here
with an Albanian spy
who is taking pictures of towers and smokestacks.

(RF & BS)

Elizabeth Ferrero

GEOGRAPHY

It was Easter at the year's beginning
the weight of winter
on the handle-bars of my bike,
then June, July, and August, sometimes even September
down into the valley.
The air is the same, I wouldn't know about the sky,
the rustle is missing; it has flown among the station's
wisteria.
A space recalls
bunches of grapes like handfuls of earth.
The taste is the drought that approaches
meadows in bloom among crusted fields,
down here sometimes a pear-tree, never ripe,
apples on the ground . . . the buzzing of hornets
a frog in the well with the chipped verdigris rim.

You don't wait any longer whenever a whistle
rises
how many times will do — I wouldn't know
if the road, if the day's tint
gone mad so long before,
if the address is no longer the same.
What's missing is
        a superfluous scene,
a study in black and white, even the train
assumes more than it needs
without effort.

The distance is bright; still today
there are corners locked up
in the cellar a cat has to come and go without opening
the door, beneath everything
the same center
stretched more to one side (for now).

                                     (RF & BS)

THE ONLY BIT OF SHADE IN THE PLACE

Whose step suspended at the beginning?   I heard
the rhyme dissonant
as puppies in the shade.
It took a straw hat to break
the enchantment of a polyphonic
sky
flattened by a still flatter sea
to linger a little on a wall
that lowers
the tone
but doesn't flee prefixes stated
openly because a stare is
all
here.

One starts again when one leaves
to wait
for the sea to stop a while to
catch its breath or listen soon
to evening's litanies.
The colors smell worn
but do not tire,
actually what stands out is a water-color palette
tasting more of spring
than summer if it weren't for the sea,
which is there to make itself remembered and not
to remember
the evening.

To accumulate summers like postcards
IN THE PLACE to
leaf through THE ONLY like the abacus BIT OF SHADE
in the silence that
jars (him too)
but it doesn't know why there are no seagulls
in the sky
"it's a secret that skims
without declaring itself:

it's the presence that counts"
then
evening will come with closed eyes
one might as well let oneself be cancelled
as in "closing"
foreign or *domestic*
now that the sun drowns in the horizon.

(JY &RF)

YELLOW AND WHITE

I wish you would come back
with the flowers and everything
even without spring
              even in winter. snow
              is the laughter of the poor and
              the very young and it changes
a bare tree how many
longings leafed through and torn by the wind
              but still on the mimosa branch
              because yellow and white agree
              in winter
and then it raises
silt
in the vase
              out of snow the snow
              pursues
              the dilated
thought
and it's   the snowflakes that fall
first
              to cover one's mouth
              because behind it is continuous
              yellow

(JA & RF)

Gilberto Finzi

THREE FORMULAS OF DESIRE

I

Danae /   stuck on the bier
I dream of autumn's
probable swift flora

maybe the result of savage causes

maybe the nausea of those freebound

otherwise you think
of things done differently / of soon
ravaging the authority-blessed benches
breaking eggs in 15 minutes
a hired mourner slow global fame

on the sea
        the ailing sea

among clustered algae and treacherous sands
mystery-shoals, rolling tides of Rhodes

I stood at the helm of our deathbarge

miraculous Danae and son

fatal lashing of salt and waves
feces and boles opposing gusts
disguises of the Church
that had escaped/deceived us

it incites riots / the sea a bed
heavy care fills the sail
on the bier steered by Eros/Thanatos
present out of jealousy —

Die a persona impersonate yourself

2.

Cannibals of sleep, work-eaters
dressed in coveralls, greedy greedy

with whales in their palm or in the weave
living worthily in synthesis, proofs

of Trojan twigs, of
Egyptian asps, Achaean yarrows

on golden chains, rubber masks
— like shoes, soles, boots —
where on earth?

a languid crow a thread
of strangling silk —   thug? —

and overflowing in glass the
carnivorous bird

close the window
— quickened noise, necklace of sand —

(much of the yr. is thanks to you)

many of us destroyed in sight of the desert

we had to help ourselves to skeletons
appearing in poison and dullness of mind
on the plant of the betrayed stone

(Jarry wrote on a bicycle you suppose)

3.

Tattered cells breaking down on the heart
                                                    of the powerful

ambushed by the microbe of the columns

beneath stone skins felids dragons

without anyone knowing the month the day

of thirst, ripened
in steps, stages, ellipses
in mathematical death
about to begin making the gold
                         of

studded stars

fallen into theory
(the continents?)

                       I was alone, exhausted, land
sterile,
     miracle-cured by lava, in
a worthless time, in unreal time
computed on record or tape

               on the rim of Etna
tired weak mystery black coupling
where *les neiges d'Antan* were
shat on the man you were/used to be/are
might be/might have been/architect of yourself

comicmystery / chain / poor people

where Tancredi / Godfrey / Rinaldo
Arganti / Clorinda and other
                       NONHEROES
would have slaughtered the trees

final (Brechtian) crime

                                    (WSDP)

Andrea Genovese

THE ASTRONAUT

I rediscover the mourning
of nocturnal shadows
on the earth, the coldness
of grass and stone,
my resigned stray-dog
sadness transplanted
to this nutshell.
So light
I feel tipsy
and the space-ship dances
over my head like
the tavern-ceiling
to old men hoarse
from wine and tobacco,
quarreling at their games.
I too have my magic
bond with cards
horoscope-route
traced on a map
of a Galaxy swarming
with microbes and gangrene.

A band of bluish light
detaches itself
from the satellite's
cone of shadow.
Below, fumes of gray dust
are steaming,
craters, marshy
silences: each shape
rebinds itself to the primeval
cells. And overhead hangs a sky
in which nothing happens
any more.

On the cottonwool of nothing
the sun's roar
dies away; the planets
scarcely etch
a silent trail
of ellipses, side-slipping.
Also, ordinates and abscissas
of these giants
all meet at one point
and that X is already time,
human solitude.

A little while ago I flew over
a small planet which
the sun's rays were striking
slantwise: a vast zone
of veinings glittered blue
as a sea and farther on
there were green streaks as if
for a subterranean springtime.
A shiver passed
in a fine dusting of lights
a slow torment
of memories, a deformed
prism of earth images.

The flash that glimmered
from your eyes
I find it again dazzling
desolate galaxies.
Around me dances
a reflection from a mirror's
caprice
with which memory fumbles
and like a stubborn child
revolves it above me.
In this way is forecast
the dissolution of gas
that pursues me, the worn-out
charnel-house of the void:

          the Beyond will be perhaps
          a delirium
          of maddened asteroids.

                    (RF)

ANAMNESIS

so evanescent those Martians
they almost seemed unreal to him
maybe they didn't come from Mars
but instead from another planet
not even part of our solar system
otherwise how to explain the extreme difficulty
of understanding their way of speaking those grunts
and hissing sounds
"the dream" he kept repeating "is"
and there they stood dangling their heads impatiently
piercing him with their X-ray glances
that probed his blood
while, panting, he consulted the manual
of spatial polyglot
"the dream" he repeated "is
a slow falling gentlemen into the void
a plunge I mean but slow you understand
here we have studied the phenomenon at length
with quite clever intuiting
for all that it seems to me we have not yet
scientifically penetrated the value of the fall"
but he certainly did not want to irritate those distinguished guests
they might ask his superiors if he had gone too far
"the dream you understand"
he repeated riffling the pages of the manual
while they dangled their heads impatiently
if indeed those cement blocks with two slits
for rays were heads

it was no laughing-matter
if he didn't succeed in making himself understood
that damned manual was no help at all and neither were
the parentheses squares and circles the mess of lines and dots
the printed sawteeth and the collages
something quite different was needed but what
"I was telling you gentlemen about the fall which we earthlings
link to the apple
but at this point gentlemen the discourse
would get too long without taking into account the fact that at present
it's not at all certain that Adam
fell on the Earth was it not perhaps we ask ourself
a geogalactic error basically a metaphysical swindle"
by this time he was wheezing waving the dictionary
cowed by their evasive animal stares
they didn't understand him they weren't Adamites.

(RF)

Amedeo Giacomini

FRAGMENT

...And to say what I am not
even if it costs blood
(of words, or even of intentions)
telling of the algebraic Ulysses
who rounds off angles and unsaddles them
for an alibi new to falsehood
and of the mason who entrusts his fate
to the plumb line and abandons it
as if the wind were enough to give it direction,
and that I am not compassionate toward myself or others
that I am only what I am
in my desire to be while I am not...

(JP)

HERBS, CLOTS, BLOCKS,

contorted amoebas, extensive mirror
night waits, decaying, for time to pass...
The obsessive shadow, eagle or automaton,
the black slough that nourishes the mind
exhausts the present in axioms.
Cunning serpents crowd the embankments,
your body slopes from perverse anxiety,
piling up refuse, deliriums, phantasms
under the shoulder in electric spasms.
In sleep the senses' turmoil spreads,
claims sewers, censures, decompensations.
Was it useless than for you to exile yourself
among mirrors, exegete of miasmas?
In tangible filth,
which makes your hair and fingers greasy,
you expiate in slime your insane life!

(JP)

THE NIGHT ARMS ARCADIAN STRUGGLES:

"More, love, more. . ."
Where are tower, moat, defences?
"Praise the lemur, the frog, be strong,
if your future is rotting in the past,
horrifying feast of dead leaves!"
Will the reward be deceit or fate's decree?
From roses I infer harshness, straining,
ugly with blood and soot,
after the groans, brawls, love affairs,
but the evil still in wait for me is vile,
to ask life for an accounting,
a life husked in useless days between fingers,
the cry in the desert, wine, wound. . .

(JP)

Alfredo Giuliani

BLUE LIKE FRIDAY

How must I behave, I asked so as to know (to have,
instead, one asks for) whether the black wing would finally
                                be destroyed.

The astrologer said: (destiny): generally good,
it will probably happen and you must not regret it, the sickle
                                      moon
sideways and radiant, considering the era, (floating in the meadow
in full daylight), a small satisfaction, the position of Uranus
could decide or the winter which comes from spaces
coincides with some friend or relative, don't hesitate to do it,
procuring notoriety for them (noise of shears from the garden),
with the aim of discrediting it, keep the talisman with you
                                      at all times.

it will be a rather monotonous month.

And the psychiatrist said: (apropos of the dream): the image
of the child with turds in hand is the world
wide luminous empty narrow dark full elevated deep
mobile impure immobile filthy contagious disgusting
welcoming menacing limitless sad
poisonous sticky decomposed penetrating

physiognomous ignominious numinous is the world
bloody sharp spermatic soft terrifying
dissolute dizzy embezzling metamorphic
vengeful sly obstinate enamored (let it be clear)
until (you finish penetrating the penetration) you return
to the contemplation (the gate is gracefully draped with ivy) and
I replied: what lovely peace here, where objects excavate
their surfaces: I wanted to turn round, but it fled weeping.

                                                  (RF & BS)

GREY CLEARINGS LIGHT UP

In the lots for sale a gang of kids
preys on grasshoppers, and plants
handkerchief-topped sticks among the thistles.

Work is in progress behind the fence,
it gains with the thud of cement mixers,
drips with the asphalt,
peels the sky with the electric saw.
Razed to the ground the mute tower.

From my shell of ruin burst dove-notes.

The fleeing band leaves a happy scent.
There on the villas the sun's setting,
and the gray clearings light up,
the river darkens, a wind blows
that neither ravages nor stings.
The red lights keep watch at the corners of the castle.

(CF)

BIRTHDAY

At thirty,
untangle your rumpled thoughts
while the sky darkens
between noon and winter,
the antennae march toward the North
and your ear gets dusty.
At every bend, a swarm of purple
angels leads the way.
There a disarmed scarecrow
on the field's breast;
there on the hills' back, in sorrowing
figures, harsh and strong olive trees,
two by two,
twined in tender dialogue.

A whiff and the earth slopes,
a voluble sky dissolves in the eye.
Where the past holds out,
guilt makes its nest,
the long night dazzles the blood,
and the woods have sinister dreams.

When the heart is lame and the hand
worries the love rope tight around
the neck, suffering's enigma
squeaks in a well.
When you say: "The mind is disintegrating,
life is sad with chatter."
it's an arc of wind between light
and rain.
Oh, the rooster that crows in your sleep!
The sacred garden was locked in an iron cage,
the tongue squeezed
between a coin and a wall.

Behind the syllables that the Enemy rends
the scourge of dead souls comes and goes,
and the house welcomes a disheartened moon.

Let me suffer for you the descent
of rich autumn: beyond my thought-
bridges I will wind a road
up to the most inaccessible spring.
If it's too late to rake our luck
with the yellowed minute,
I will come by the power of creation.

There: thunder shouts in my veins,
the hedge opens.
Let lovers refuse to yield to pollen
and let the wolf wear grandmother's cap,
I will come to clip the space
of fresh habits
and to tell you the insect's voyage
in the wheat-field.

Who remembers the leaf stretched
toward the cold of the gate?
the long bundled eyes of the year?
I will always come
to fill the empty thorn in my heart
and to rise again.

         (CF)

Renato Gorgoni

THE GARBAGE VISE

Here is an example of one of the many ecological "traps" in which we find ourselves: one per cent of the garbage that Milan has to burn is made up of bags containing the garbage... There is great interest therefore in ongoing research which is engaged in finding rapidly degradable plastic materials. This research has recently produced some initial results...

(from the newspapers)

> The problem is to find the perfect casing
> for our tons of garbage
> a little sack that would be destructible
> a real inflammable object
> refuse of the refuse
> and then once serene we could start to sully
> with subtle mephitic poisons
> the air, water, fauna, flora
> we could feel free to dirty
> we could enclose and throw out
> garbaging-up we will rejoice
> with the drainage of factories
> toluene and chrome to give back
> some tone to the rivers and sea
> there is after all the perfect little sack
> with children we can be polite dandies
> we'll defile in yellow gloves
> dredging up bacchanals of the chamberpot
> our personal excrement
> patent made in Italy
> is an exceptional patent
> little girls' urine in silver phials
> our life will make sense.

(MJC)

CAMERA OBSCURA

to Ugo Mulas

The earth now envelops you
in its soft darkroom
after the final framing the photos
begin to curl up due to the torrid
finish, its rotten vapor
does not speak of Brera's grey evenings
it does not bring back the clicks of far-off
fantastic close-ups
of wide-open panoramas

                here a sky of trees
ready for battle rises up against
the ramparts of the city's houses
and I am here upon this very earth I live
while death embraces you and you sleep
in her deep eyes
and laugh at the days of great cries
between your white teeth like some
ancient Phoenician warrior's

                the leaves rot lightly
patiently they cradle you
after the final framing
in your light darkroom

(MJC)

Margherita Guidacci

from **ALL SAINTS' DAY**

III

I have often thought: this is
The year's real end and Apocalypse
With its brown and gray, two empty bezels,
All the colored gems that stared at us
Before, extinguished. The world is
Dissolved in these rotten ferments
Of death. The water carries the earth
Away from the mountains, leaving
the stones naked, the wind carries the leaves
Away until the final dryness
Of the trees. Nothing remains but to hope
For the time when there will no longer
Be anything to lose. Already under
The anguish of flesh the skeleton
Shows and reaffirms the harsh
And patient wait.
                This is
The end, not December with crystal
Skies, the Star of the East
And men kneeling to adore
The Child. In silence—though
Hidden from the world—hope will revive
With the seed under the snow. But twice
In these days when earth itself
Resembles a scene from the Last Judgment
He who will return is recalled
To us from the altar: no longer a child
To save us, but an adult to judge
The quick and the dead, to exclude any new
Redemption. Then time's hinges
Will turn, huge and bleak,
And eternity shall be. You alone,
Saints, will dare to fix it with your gaze.

V

I have many memories of November: too many
Times now the sky's cold Sagittarius has drawn his bow
Above my life. And I find again many things in the past
With a painful meaning they didn't have at the time,
Or that I didn't see. Days
Of adolescence and the short vacations
At the beginning of this month: I roamed
The countryside, among damp leaves;
It was fun to trample and kick them
Ahead of me, heedless
Then as the wind. I searched for
Ferns on the paths' edge, happy
With their bitter scent, their varied
Designs. I saw
Reddish bushes pale little by little
To inert gray,
Hailed the first
Ice-star that appeared on top
Of a mud-puddle. In stinging
Air, where every bird-cry
Was a blade, I exulted
More in my freedom than under
The summer sun . . .
                     Then came a wartime November.
Streams fell from the mountains,
Covering the streets where tanks
Of three foreign armies
In pursuit had dug
Deadly ruts, often debouching
Into bomb-craters. In the invaded
Earth, among people
Bowed and scattered under the storm,
Impending winter bared the depths
Of each evil . . .
                Later I found myself

One November far
From my country: I see again the deserted
Beach at Howth, a sombre sky
And the sparse and livid gleam there
Seemed to rise
From under the sea, like a malevolent
Thought that leaped suddenly
From a heart without peace . . .

                         (RF & BS)

Armanda Guiducci

PRESENTIMENT OF SPRING

Today the thoughtless sun
seemed to take pity
and so shone in a yellow frenzy
freeing our eyes. While the haze
unfurled from pale rows of mulberry trees
low summer swarmed vigorous
and beyond the Po on the crest of bare woods
reordered time so
the pheasant's cry cut it in two.

(RF & BS)

THE ROADS OF THE WEST

Even this sky disappears
even tonight's sky
draws back from eyes from fingers
from blood that has enjoyed another light

deep blue severe irresistible
along the course of lived days
of round sacked suns
the dark winged boat of breaths
toward the curved western
void

(RF & BS)

WHERE

Roosters, threat of light, shout time
beginning again from time on hills
on unknown slopes who knows where
the sun ends, the earth, maize is born
in the dawn of their eternal embraces
after the solar night—and where
the earth begins again and the young sun
assaults the throat of birds
with the vibrations of morning.
And where where—A trolley.
It rushes out of a tunnel outside of sleep
and shakes the night-swollen windows.
The latest slaughters wake the newsstands up.
Rapid packages of fresh newsprint
give out the first odor of lilac.

Who knows where morning begins.

(CF)

PULVIS ES

Suddenly the dust makes a light
dry whirl, windmill of nothing
of infinitesimal, microscopic elements.

Ah dust is rich in energy
its kingdom is huge without limits.
Dust confounds the dead. Weds seed to seed.
It conjugates the times with deserts.
It travels the winds. The parching heat.
The land. Space, black, intact, universal.
Intolerant of voids of interstices
even between moons, among planets.

(CF)

Federico Hindermann

TOWARD THE HOLIDAYS

The boy with the knapsack on the way to school
gnaws the apple in his woolen glove
and follows, perhaps still dreaming, the track
of the last fox near home.
Here in the Jura it has already snowed
this year. Valleyward the mist
consumes the small red in his hand,
it is lost bite by bite, disappears forever.
To the North, though, on the Rhine plain
they say the sky is clear
as you turn behind the Alps far off,
but very far off, they say, and even
while I think of you here on the crest
you are in the light of elsewhere.
But where did he come from, which of these mountains,
Zimmermann, the one with the forelock,
running all the way down, world champion racer,
extravagant Swiss?
Even the swiftest
falters in the laps.
There remains the date, '93, in the snare
the forelock, like the fox's brush, a bookmark
among forgotten words.

And you who would like to live by the river,
would you at least glimpse in the mirror
the schoolboy's shadow? That red dot still?
They also say, down there
they used to throw an apple for a gift.
It rolled to the feet,
and your truelove picked it up.

(AD)

THE BIRCH AT THE HOUSE WALL

If towards evening the birch
in a gust of north wind approaches
the house wall and bends womanly
from the dark trailing her long fronds
against the panes, I do not ask her of her past,
which is enough to change the wind, and it dissolves
in hops of a titmouse among the branches
and timidly reappears
in the brighter leaves just uncurled.
The nut falls from the paws of the squirrel
pricked up to listen, he does not chase it;
the hail was lost that way, the raindrops
fell and the light in rays
around the trunk that anchored cinches
sapwood denser between ring and ring
and serves as pivot to the stars' rotation.

Some memories I would have
collected here around the burned-out bulb,
some far-off flavor to rediscover
in the glass of cold wine obscured on the table.
But when I turn even that little disappears
in the mirror of the window
where a surf already black hurls itself
against the next instant.

(AD)

Gina Labriola

ORGY
(that is, vegetable market, at Sarno)

The drunken sun
totters among the clouds
and without inhibitions
shouts
to call us all together.
We are all here,
already drunken all.
The solanaceous in pink satin
are all flushed
they drank too much.
The slim cucurbitaceous
are waiting for the surly vigilantes
to offer themselves as livid bludgeons
but the splendid round pumpkins
offer to the sun their gold buttocks.
The peppers more and more aroused
trickle their acid blood
on lettuce leaves.
Peppers, splendid children of the sun,
who are you? Red green yellow flags?
And of what country?
No! We are not flags
we are phalluses erect.
Latex and honey
from shameless wanton figs
pour on their modest leaves.
Oh chaste fig leaves!
On the sidewalk the cabbage offers himself.
His cousin, the cauliflower,
is a priest
fat and with a white voice.
In my heart there is a tuft of purple pistils
held in a claw of thorns.
"Open up," says the sun,

pouring wine down my throat,
"my thistle, if you don't make up your mind
you won't be either flower or fruit
and you won't find even a tapeworm
to eat your heart."
I know.
But what can I do?
I am waiting for someone to swallow me up,
but with all my thorns.

(EP)

JOHN

You didn't look at me
when I brought you
in the folds of my kerchief
sheep's cheese
and unleavened bread
and the current
(the Sinnai's or the Jordan's)
made your feet turn livid.
You didn't look at me
when I brought you water
to quench the parched thirst
of your self-denial
and the desert dust
split your lips
and your prophetic shout
dried up your throat.
You didn't look at me
when I gave you wine
between the prison bars
and you gave ear
to another voice
and strained to perceive it

between the songs and the music
and the beat of the dance
and the anathema
filled your mouth with voluptuousness
as though it were love
it tore your insides
as though it were jealousy.
You didn't look at me
when they left you
among the feast's left-overs
the trays of food
and the overturned cups
you too on a tray
livid like a party's aftermath
I dried with my apron
the wine and the blood
and your followers hadn't arrived yet
to recompose you.
Alone with me
but your eyes lifeless.
And now for you they shoot firecrackers
fireworks
at midnight
and lovers find omens in them
they've forgotten the dances
and the feast of love and rage
when you died for her.
Yes, you look at me now
but with a glassy stare.
And after the fair we too
among the drowsy sheep
the tired donkeys
we too feast
drinking wine from pitchers of clay.
There is one more dance
with her percale shirt
a peasant Salome
dances among poppies
and ears of wheat
for you who knew only
desert thorns.

Herod smokes his cigar
counting the money in the collection box
he won't cut off your head
this time
after the fair.
He'll put you back in your niche
next to Saint Anthony.
You look at me finally
you come to meet me
with open arms
tottering in the procession.
Your mouth of chalk
has no more anathemas of love
or incandescent prophecies
the lamb of God
they've eaten it roasted
the sins of the world
not even blood has cleansed them.
You're no longer thin and smooth
but there is the band from Molfetta
perhaps even the merry-go-round
for your name day.

(EP)

Mario Lunetta

IN RESPECT OF TRADITION

(for Maria Pia)

Windshield fouled to a ruinous
graveyard of insects, the rainbowed coleoptera
escaped it by a breath and a shiver, the squashed
abdomen of a wasp leaks thick fluids onto the glass,
the countryside beyond the yellow smear
repels daisies and camomile like a sea —
there is no hesitating, now: direct
attack and swallowing up the damned asphalt.
Your smile has three teeth missing, half-hidden
by the back of the violet hand,
as you see, the *seventese* continues, certainly
wings get broken here inside the car,
the north winds are weak, as the weather
service informs us, the wrist of the undersigned
leaning on the axis of the steering-wheel, has no
ambition to rise to the helm of the rudder,
rein in your impatience, twenty kilometers still to go
and you'll climb onto the hydrofoil. At Elba the same hotel-room
we had last year awaits us. Here is the real reason
for my childish embarrassment,
of these homicidal *raptus* to the injury
of the scattered hymenoptera. I am, however,
disposed to ask your pardon: as for the rest, we'll see afterwards. Or
                              tomorrow. Or who knows.
Provided it's afterwards: after, also, this unnatural speed,
haste or rashness as the case may be. If we go looking
for disasters, help me at least to sweep my aching memory clean
of the burdensome memory of the friend
dead forty-eight hours ago of lung cancer, since, as you know,
order is not my strong suit, my archives leave
too much to be desired. Please give me
the Clausewitz that is lying on the back seat,

if you still hold to the idea that it's nice to spare me certain
                                                    enormous jobs.
I have not yet lost my personal war,
but for such meagre returns it's dubious if it's worth the candle
to fight valiantly on all thirteen fronts,
not even respecting the ritual Tet truce . . .

                                                                             (RF)

Giorgio Luzzi

ALBORADA DEL GRACIOSO

>   Let's get close to the fire so we can see
>   what we're saying.
>   Quoted from the Bubi di Fernando Poe

He's talking in his sleep. He says, "Oh, yeah,
that's the way it happened." staying awake, not so much to listen
as to understand, rather,
what was being said, the other day, of the fact
that one or the other, there is one, it's important,
who, however, takes you out of the shit

                    Since, then,
this is the way he talks, and not differently, and his voice
                    is wise,
and strangely clean, like that of a sick woman, without the stridency
of our phonetic border vocation
                    and the things he says
finally are true, not because they're in some way verified
but simply because they were said and also because
now there is one who listens as in a telephone call
breathing darkness from dilated eyes
and the fire to which one draws close so as to
see what's being said isn't needed
                    For this reason
it's the eyes that want to
              take her and make a nest for her
to attain the arms, straw, coffee on the night-table,
to slaughter the alarm-clock, to enter
together into a different notion of history,
this yes,
better than hers and mine.

                                                      (JP & AN)

Giancarlo Majorino

DOUBLE OCCUPATION

This 1,000 lira bill
under the foot of the wind
on the lake is it me?
off schedule far
from the office powdered
meat not suitable
for eating
wood in the trunk or debarked in stacks
or roughed out with an ax or split
this torn bill is it me?
> maps sky-blue seas
> without asterisks or signs of fish
> simple salted, dried, smoked,
> the Poet's house was hidden
> by clusters of sparkling stores
> gases spectrally pure
> and slaughtered birds (lard)
> slept on the marble table
> he wrote "continuous sheets
> of rolled steel, in strips
> lukewarm, red-hot"
> the Poet traveling salesman for glues
> of animal origin
> ears pierced by sirens
> of detained transatlantic steamers hands
> hidden and protected by gloves

under those sirens I walked
among stores like a paltry amount
on long checks with irregular
signatures with endorsement unknown
and lacking a date abused
by the tellers because there aren't enough zeros
> essential oils of myrrh, thyme,
> mint, sage, clary, rosemary
> slowed the Poet down started up

"continuous sheets of rolled steel,
in strips, hot-rolled, cold-rolled, semi-cold-rolled"
with glues of animal origin
I brushed sky-blue maps
seas on factories and walls
of lined-up workers "excuse my back"
and there where ostentatious neglect
betrayed betrays (and tomorrow?)
exemptions from gold and privileges
I watched with face between pillows
of double lines of loaded stores
the painted tie with beautiful stripes
the writing-desk with mahogany and leather
the curtains swollen by a soft breeze at the lake
I appeared to be a man of importance I had a respectable
felt hat on my head a sweater on my chest
my teeth whitened by toothpaste
a double profession increases war and peace.

(LS)

ANNIVERSARY

Cold wind, my wife is dead, what really matters though... boy,
                                                                          it's cold. It's the wind
If my wife died would I write this way? I don't have a wife.
Lumumba is dead and I have nothing to write.
So many months have passed.
Few; but so many stories on that news, so much indignation after
that; we're putting up a monument for him in Bologna.
But even here it's cold (you won't get away with this allusive line;
better to describe the lazy ways you have, the false maturity which
is complacency, this allusive paunch which is really bulging).
It's just that we watch whoever has the latest thing.
Of this, however, I'm sure: the poets of his land will sing of
                                                                               Lumumba.
And what do we do?
the heirs of classical culture,
racial pride, the heirs of nazism,
what do we say?
words which, when written, seem like speeches blessing the
                                                     armies which conquered,
shall destroy, and now are plundering.

                                                                                             (LS)

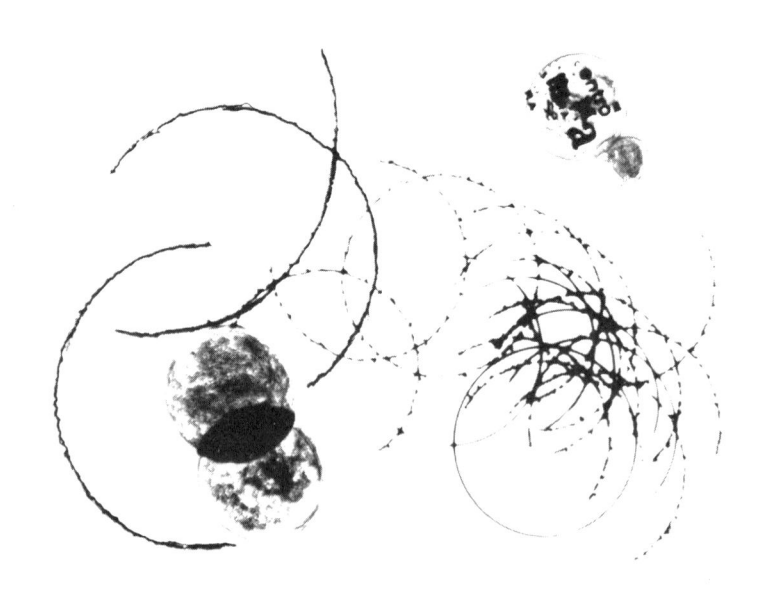

Giorgio Manacorda

ENCLOSURES

the storm petrel on the tallest islands
the flat expanse of water: the hawk's
fear in the emptiness

of a change of light

*

voyage on the lake and the search
dies in winter's dog-days
turn your head and the water

looks like snow

*

if the mountains form a barrier
empty skies and the fear
of finding corpses

preserved in the urn of light

*

involuntary enclosures
rubble a disturbance
jolts the horizon

to the boundaries of the water and the tombs

*

islands in the lake the fisherman
uses miles of netting to divide
graves among the little girls

(WSDP)

ANTIWORLDS

wingbeat
exultant on the hard lake: winter
brings   on dizziness and its impact

is awaited like bad luck

           *   *   *

curses flee the open countryside
time has fixed designs and the river
dams and shears

antiworlds
born after every departure

           *   *   *

don't ever laugh   toothed
sectors butcher maleoli

bone-clicks and the fruit

of ten years' sowing
drops green from the belly

           *   *   *

the ever innocent monster
thrives in hollow dwellings

and his scythe will scrape out your heart

                                       (WSDP)

EAST-WEST

hyperbole and condemnations have gladdened
the splits of light
rectangles   green   amaranth   collage

and you too will become an enemy
like all the young girls of ancient Egypt
lost at the source

the night on the eastern waters
telling its proverb
of the hot pot and cold fire

                     *   *   *

I have seen cats and serpents
preening the forked hide
and the fata morgana with rattles

filling the desert
and the great-eyed bat weaving
through the caves considering

the gifts of rats and vampires

                     *   *   *

den   hope   digestion
in the cave that consumes
searches out and attacks

the caravans of the sick have passed,
and the long slow trains
orphanages   bedrooms   hospitals

happy that life is a dream
for anyone with his organs in place
and head off center

                     *   *   *

if the leaves you have on your eyes
are for fighting and the waterfront
will be different than the known water-edge

you'll gather unfleshed shells
the mollusk burned by dust
will leave you in sundown's green

fondling bones and towers
notched by sand-signs

     * * *

ancient halberds tombstones flowers
colors green dominant

gulf like the scooped hollow ubicumque
of Philippine women
in the eyes of fish metamorphosis

where embraces slither
through water tendrils
and bakelite flowers

in the household acquarium

     * * *

the stone pearl grey green rotten
like the fish-eye on ice
the guest is like love the cemeteries

have milestones along the paths
tombs and peach blossoms
while springtime corrupts

bundles of light eyes
in long plaster necklaces
mouldgreen hopeblack

     * * *

peach blossoms inside the caves
where great ugly birds loom forth

augury in the magnolia heart
dry crumbly plant
with its roots

knotted to the travelling foot

        *   *   *

the stars droop their long necks
in imitation of paintings
now pale green where it once was azure

cheatblue   falsehoodblue   prepare yourself
the moon is swollen
and the voyage in those coastal waters begins again

        *   *   *

for the green sun-bred light
apricosen in bloom

and the executioner isn't here
just now

(WSDP)

Giorgio Mannacio

TWO PASSAGES OF HISTORY

Sad as the arse-end alley
of some apartment house on Sunday—
what made you want to learn an alphabet
so long ago? The scribes will inherit
the earth and its splendors.
They will screw your wife: there's a motif
that eternally returns.
When we've all lost our memories
poppies will bloom amid the tiles
of the temples. The Chinese laughed
taking off their shoes
in Caracalla's bath.

To what does the jellyfish
rotting at San Nicola turn
our thoughts? Gratian, says the guide,
lies under here. He got his throat cut
at Lyons, at night. And others too—
Berengarius for example authorized
the market in this piazza and the Germans
shot forty-two refugees
at Fondo Toce one June. On the stone
that marks the boundary
a whore sits waiting.

(PB)

HAMLET'S WILL

Proof of paternity is not lacking.
The waves of Elsinore carried a bottle
to the lad far from home
with a coded message. He knew Latin,
his mind full of fantasy and his speech
like a blade unsheathed.
The night is a funnel, Ophelia a comet
that condenses and spawns in the frozen sky.
Every kingdom (remember!) is built
on dung, fine gold only if
Croesus & Co. touch it
with skeleton hands.

(PB)

THE CAPTURE OF ROME

This is the way Rome ends. Spitted
from beak to rump the Capitol geese
revolve over the coals. And the Vestals?
When the wine is down to the dregs, just say so
(in the Latin of the Gospels perhaps)
and the miracle is ready, behind the door.

Sic transit gloria mundi
and the waters of Boffalora
that sometimes carry a child of ruin
right to the door. Nevertheless
bless the wine and what they call lust
and in summer the smile of watermelon.

(PB)

Dacia Maraini

HIS FOOT ON THE SAND

I looked at his swollen foot
exposed on the gray sand and
the way the water covered it with little
clear waves, I wanted to kiss his mouth
but I stood still staring at his foot
and the disgust with myself and my face
sort of blonde, rather stiff
that swollen foot, covered and uncovered by the sea
my self-disgust, weak and weary
in the coil of my intestines
I couldn't stop it nor vomit it
I think perhaps I touched his
cheek with mine sniffing
his usual odor of sun-tan oil
maybe I even licked his chin
with the tip of my tongue
but I stood still and stared
at the hump-backed foot and the water washing it
the nausea of being the thing I was
leaped from my throat like a sob

(EP)

BOVARY IN A TWO-PIECE BATHING SUIT

Desires are deep and wavy humps,
I don't know when I was pierced by the green
finger of an impatient boy, on the branches of the
cherry tree, toward summer, your head, father,
venomously close to the bathroom window,
thieves came that night, you

fired in the air, steep Saint Flavia
and patches of rocks on July's polluted
sea, I was already and utterly an object,
all I remember is a bony sail and the hooks'
bloody wake in the white-chequered
water, I don't know whether it was that boy, Peter
or someone else, the clear tongue sought
my ear, seated, singing, I was a
confused animal with no heart, no fingers
to understand and touch, where, when did we
deceive one another? I deceitful already
but cowardly, ready to separate
truth from the true and you blond sporty
with your fear upside down turned into scornful
heroism, without ever guessing that true
courage lies elsewhere, concealed in a sober
fair perception of things, there were
twenty eggs in a row on the marble table
and a dead man's hat, you smiled at
the absurd murky incantations of popular
superstition, I remember also a tremulous Bovary
in a two-piece bathing suit, the three of us on a boat,
the sail's sharp jerks, the water bristly
windy, I kept turning away not to discover
her flesh on yours, I was thirteen
perhaps, the salty green made my eyes water
I leaned against rolled up
shrouds, the sail's tight wind-bag against
my mouth, the three of us nearly end in Tunis,
the Bovary woman stamping her feet against the boat's
belly, laughing victorious, you restrained her
keeping an eye on me, but already the black
tulip of sweet hypocricy was born, we
you and I, were secret accomplices, the mast
creaked, the sail flapped fertile and obtuse,
far very far away the warm fatal ridge
of Mount Saffron, you, the woman
and I were fixed forever in a
shiny mannerist painting

(EP)

KOBE

"Whoever loves life, shall go from death to death," the
amaranth monk's morning song crept
through sliding paper and light wood walls, in
a Japanese concentration camp, you white
I white, the rice-fields frozen, the morning blackbirds
hopping about, "don't bend to seize the morning-glory,
it blooms for only an hour," Kobe south of Tokyo,
among calm waters, grey snakes, the hoarse sound
of frogs, the horizon dipped in oil, we
slid down the embankment sifting, careful with
our hands, through bloody gauzes, empty bottles,
singed documents, entrails of dead animals,
"time is a bloc of insubstantial clouds,"
the opaque green voice, threatening touched our
ears naked and numb, "the past and the
present and the future are only feeble inventions
of pragmatic minds," the monk lifted himself on his
heels, brushing the mats with his chest, and
our rice? He lifted his eyes to the faded
ceiling, his strong fingers twined on his thighs,
his mouth half-open and arched, "hunger will have you
like death," his clean bronze forehead, wrinkled
his knees sharp and icy, "until you
free yourselves from the senses' deception," from
the boy that just died bed-bugs escaped drawn up in
columns, silver-white rice and yellow turnips
hurriedly swallowed, you washed cloths in a tub
sterile eater of sun-flower seeds, your hands
swollen, your body dried up, "all pain
is illusory," he whispers, "only the roses of
contemplative joy are unmoving and perfect,"
nimble and pollished, the monk pointed at the
gold simulacra's dark and symmetric forms and
its smell of fermented rice, cane wine, dried
fish, mine was a liquid stupor, and yours
a timid dark pain, "life is vanity, we
snow shadows on the snow," the accustomed thin voice,
the crossed legs, the fasting monk's bare and paper-like

chest, we asked aloud for rice
for our cold mouths, the body
of the praying man rose on the red
pillows, his face enraptured, "but can't you renounce,
life is mud, meditate," the will to rebel
had vanished, humiliated and empty waiting for the slow
sound of peace, we gave the hard and hollow sky
a low and stolid look, without love.

(EP)

Elsa Morante

SUNDAY EVENING

Through the pain of sick wards
and of all prison walls
of barbed-wire camps, of convicts and their keepers,
of ovens Siberias and slaughter-houses
of marches solitudes drunkenness and suicides
and the leaps of conception
the sickly sweet taste of the seed and the dead,
through the innumerable body of pain
theirs and mine,
today I reject reason, majesty
that denies the last grace,
and I spend my Sunday with madness.
Oh pierced prayer of elevation,
I claim for myself the guilt of the offense
in the vile body.
Stamp your grace
on my ill-grown mind. I receive you.

And the small carnage begins again.
The sweat nausea the cold fleshy fingertips the bones' agony
and the round of wonderful abstractions
in the horror of stripping away flesh.
The usual deadly female peacock called Scheherezade
unfurls her wheel of stabbing pains,
feathers and flowers suddenly petrified
in the giddiness of colors against nature, a lacerating lynching
with sharp stones. No way out.
The range of the limitless is another prison law
more perverse than any limit. But still
beyond a glacial era the daily norm
resurfaces at intervals with its poor domestic face
while the blend of nature's kingdoms
melts the veins in waves like childhood's first menses
until the lymph is burned away. The carnal fever is consumed.
Conscience now is only a moth beating against the deathly dark
seeking a thread of substance. Summer is dead.

Farewell farewell destinations addresses popes bestiaries
            and numberings,
Via della Scimmia, Piazza Navona, Avenue of the Americas.
Farewell measures, directions, five senses. Farewell slavish duties
            slavish rights slavish judgments.
Take refuge blindly on the other side, hells or limbos, it
            doesn't matter,
rather than find yourself back in your disgusting domicile
where you're crushed between walls soiled by painted canvases
recognizable as rags and dust of degraded Sindons.
The floor is a bloody mud boiling again
in the rooms, disintegrating ossuaries, in the last lightning flash
of a misshapen brass plate, where lemons
swell to plastic balls. And from the mirror
with dusty eye-sockets something alien but at the same time
close, intimate, stares at you, dark fish-scale beyond every
            incarnation,
that also denies the skeleton and the whole business
of geneses and epiphanies
of tombs and Easters. Don't try the twisted ruinous itinerary
of the stairs, that is for you an ascension of centuries,
and above, below, there is always Hell.
The decayed sky is the low ragged tent
of the earthly leper-house. And the Mozartian flute
is a malign hopping that beats back
all the way into your eye-bulb its trivial mimicry
of an obsessive arithmetic that has no other meaning . . .
No further sky's exposed. The thousand-petaled lotus doesn't open.
You're all there is here. There's nothing else.
Be present at this. And stop calling on
dead lovers, dead mothers.
Stripped bare, poorer still than you, they don't frequent this
or other dimensions. Their final habitation
remains in your memory alone.

Memory memory, house of pain
where through great rooms and deserted galleries
an uproar of loudspeakers keeps repeating
(the mechanism is bewitched) always the bitter point
of the Eli Eli without an answer. The shriek of the boy

who leaps blinded by the sacred evil.
The young assassin raving in the mad dormitory.
The cropped Christian litany in the hospital
storeroom, around the old dead Jewess
who pushed away the cross with her small delirious hands.
WITHOUT THE COMFORTS OF RELIGION. This house is
                                        full of blood,
but the blood itself, all blood, is only spectral vapors
like the mind that bears witness to them.
And when the hour of requiem arrives for you, it will be like
                                      this through those cries.

The desecrated Sunday declines now
the plague-moons are already sinking
the thorny hedge buds again, your senses chime in five voices.
Hurry again, hurry to meet your usual poor tomorrows,
your usual death-doomed body.
It's supper-time. Oh hunger for life, feed yourself
again on the daily substance of slaughters.
Be born again to forms to confidences and arbitrary choruses
to consciousness
to health
to the order of dates
to your place.

No Revelation. (Even if the play is illegal,
it always depends on the collective factory of free will).
No sin (The machine designed for torture
isn't guilty of the tortures, oh poor sinners).
And no special grace.
(The only common grace is patience
up to the consummation's amen).
Go away content. Absolved, absolved, though backsliding.
Good evening, good evening.
This Sunday too is over.

                                                                            (RF & BS)

MY BEAUTIFUL POSTCARD FROM PARADISE

I had my passport, with the official visa of the world Academy
 of Higher Chemistry
signed by Doctors and Shamans with university degrees.
But the first armed guard I found in front of the barred
 entrance of the Bard
was a dead (murdered) Aztec king
who screamed at me as follows:
"We don't admit transients here unless they're stowaways or
 illegal expatriates. Get back!"
Which is why I never crossed the borders of anybody's earth.
As for the great beyond, only with difficulty could I get a
 glimpse in the distance
of a transparent dome suspended in calm dusk and trimmed
with gay balloons, it seemed, by a child author.
Meanwhile below me, in the lower regions, I could still see my
 newly-abandoned body
already crumbling into dust, its skeleton reduced to the simple
 sternum
giving off a faint radiance, like a gold watchband ...
The novelty of weightlessness intoxicated me like one's first
 drink at fifteen
when organs tissues veins all the passages and circulatory canals
are intact and clean in their fresh health
so the blessèd alcohol rains like equinoctial pollen straight
 to the flower's center.
Paradises! paradises! But still, continuously inside me
at the center of my sympathetic nervous system persisted, with
 abscess-like pangs, the conviction
that this Assumption was a substitute oneiric temporary one,
 like a price-tag marked way down,
and that from below in the terrestrial station my imminent
 repatriation was already officially foreseen.

 (RF & BS)

Alberto Mario Moriconi

INTERPLANETARY FLIGHT

I

Flight To The Stars

They pierced infinity, screeching,
the rectilinear astral torpedoes,
will-of-the-wisps of sidereal cemeteries.

An incandescent landing-place,
surely forbidden.
The Pillars of Hercules were torn away,
terrifying the ones who had remained on earth,
hateful to those who had tossed their souls behind
their backs, heavy with grief or shame
or cowardice, and who, pure mud, had stretched out
on the unloving earth:
convicts, beggars, cripples,
fierce self-negaters
already saved from suicide, form the rebellious crew:
earth's scum seeking to merge
with space
knights of darkness and light, pioneers
of human wreckage,

the first death-destined of the stars.

But in the torpedoes' prows
the poets
sat thoughtful and serene,
like small boys climbing
an orchard wall:
through blind flown tracks
the sinister shore
and the moment hurry.
They catapulted their spirits high above

to meet Icarus, Dante,
Cyrano:
having lived until now a pre-dawn dream
with a sad wandering eye.

The ionosphere rang
with the first wild howl,
violet at moments and soft as a September
evening, a perennial autumn
evening,
without a breath of wind or fires
of mountain charcoal-burners
or salts or resinous
scents.

Now see furtive nostalgia knocking at deaf
stony hearts, dulled by passions.
The constellations, burning far off
as never before.
Red-tailed
the dizzying astral torpedoes
fled lifeless red-hot abysses,
pelted by radiation:
perfect devices
more fragile than the ships that sailed from Palos,
steel and asbestos coffins remote-controlled
in the beyond.
The half-dead came alive again
                              alarmed.
All at once
immensity
        lacked a tumble-down
dwelling, yes, even a cell. . .a puppy,
a sparrow, the jovial
jailer,
the path under the lime-trees, a rosy
church-step,
faces, faces,
of other men's women, the neighbor's children . . .
Already evenings like that were spreading calm . . .
And perhaps at this hour day is breaking

below . . .
where they will never return.

Only those quiet believers in the prow
had cut their earthly ties.
As though Beatrice, celestial
and desirous, were leading them
from sky to sky to oriental sapphire,
to the Empyrean, to the Rose.

They wrenched away from the last weak gravity
of earth, and poised—sudden
satellites,
like balloons in the wind, adrift
from ghostly astral round-dances.
They whirled bewildered, silent,
without motors or real destination, phantom vessels,
spun through infinite cosmic space
by magic currents
radiated from who knows what dead
planet,
through infinite cosmic space.

Oh the ludicrous shells, the bloodless hearts, the little men
jousting with worlds . . .
Who suddenly discover in themselves mountains,
woods, water, soft
clouds, marine
horizons,
public gardens
with their children, splendid
neighborhoods
and voices eyes wrinkles thoughts
smiles of their city.
Who suddenly discover dawn
dawn dawn . . .
and they think of those skies,
so wildly eyed from the contesting roofs
of yesterday,
as a remote dwelling-place of liberty.

And their hate enveloped the pilots
who had sat down first in the prow.
There were some who chose instant extinction;
beside themselves and frothing at the mouth they beat beat
at portholes, others snatched their hammers,
                        and tore at their throats:
"Turn back turn back"
some implored, others commanded;
                        an unfrocked priest
stammered his rosary again.
                        Turn back! . . .
A prostrate convict
pulled out his knife . . .

No, no, the repeated rudder-lifts produced
a jolt, a thundering
at last! the Astroflash reared
reined by the helmsman's hand:
the two following shells, radio-guided,
braked too.
They overcame the magic currents
hurtled hurtled
were engulfed by the atmosphere.

Just as snow flutters above the dusky
countryside, and a solitary lamp
blinks far below,
the stars grown faint danced
in a dawn, above the horror
of the empty universe:
and a miniscule sun seemed to signal
the remaining route, a small flame, scarcely a match-glow
lit in front of the bows,
a dim cottage
           lamp.

Turn back, turn back
the frightened rabble bellowed,
the bards hymned the new-born
stellar life.
And the shells glided

over the immaculate
sand wastes of the new planet.

II

The Return

The multitude stormed the airport,
fast-moving and noisy as a brisk
hurricane,
unrestrainable as incandescent lava
pouring into a plain.
From continent to continent
the salvoes of archaic cannon resounded, the eternal bells
ringing full peals:
They're back, they're back,
sang the radio waves.

The silvery coffins unnailed,
reborn creatures emerged,
semi-gods, immortals,
                    who laughed humbly
in the native air;
cripples, beggars, failed suicides, gallows-birds,
and they laughed a different laugh at their excited
idolators, who had trampled them only yesterday.
"Tell us tell us tell us"
the crowd screamed hoarsely above the hymns and the
tearful hurrahs.

One of the crew stopped halfway down
the landing-ladder with an imperious wave
and slowly
the surrounding crush calmed down, with docile
and admiring looks,
the banks quieted:
only the cut-short breath
of the stupid tamed Hydra remained,
a distant unceasing roar.

"Mosses, lichens, snow,
                         craters, nothing...
Little of what we longed for and all the same.
Even a conquest like this
come to nothing, even this astral
escape.
Life sadder, the prison more cramped,
just so much less of the unknown left for dreaming
a heroic
mortal sortie.

The poets never looked back
but moved to the interior, signaling to us
the re-embarcation and return.
                         They were light
as feathers in their space-suits, invincible
seekers of the new, beyond death."

                                        (RF & BS)

Giampiero Neri

HUNTING AND FISHING CLUB

I

In the foreground, an abandoned Spanish elm.

After the remains of a wall, covered with creepers, a low
scrub of holm-oaks and cork-oaks and in part you recognize the
imaginary woods that continue on toward the background.
The painting, probably a forgery, is called "The warrior's
dream."

II

The place is suited to hunting, inhabited only by foxes.
In the darkest area, where, perhaps, there are also yew-
trees, near roots and on the fallen leaves, periodically you
find a woodcock. It flies at night, always following the
same course.
Other species of birds form a V in the air, behind the leader.
They are lured back with simulated companions, wooden mallards
and coots, that bob on the water.

III

There are many kinds of lures.
Whistles, screws, decoy-mirrors, are used by hunters, according to the season, but chiefly live birds.

IV

The observer orients himself by certain details. The color of
the leaves or the presence of ephemerids on the river-banks.
Strange short-lived insects, as their name indicates.
Toward the middle of the reserve lives the red hawk, hunter
by night. During the day he is hidden but sometimes he
crosses a valley or a clearing, molested by sparrows.

(RF & BS)

THE INN OF THE ANGELS

I

What became of those small black signs, image and likeness of a constant commitment?
They live in a close company, in the form of melancholy symbols, devoid of life.
I don't recall the details now. Having departed from an imaginary line, bad weather is at the door and is not about to say: "Friends, here I am."
It has already taken revenge many times, arrives executing its dangerous exercises.
How will you receive it when, turned over on its back, it pushes impatiently in front of your courtyard?
In this waiting, finally, the fact that the discourse presents itself in its own way is of little importance.
Génie littéraire hors de cause, your ants, Jean Henri, are a closed chapter.

II

In what strange country of the world will you find a mill, well-covered with moss, that moves its paddles merrily in the green water?
Of that which happened, only the names are changed. From your gate the street runs off behind the trees, in a frame of dust, and there are spots here and there, the masks of other times.
Surrounded by a large number of figures, the Greek's head maintained intact its strange suggestiveness.
Finally, it seemed useless to continue the research, to give a different explanation.
By now it was late, and it was hard to distinguish the surroundings.

III

At the small theatre, the meeting place was an inn with the traditional green-painted sign. I remember clearly its typical front, the windows of the room and a curious design, flanking the entrance, a kind of sensitive warning.
But then a great deal of interest in the performance was evident and I myself was waiting for it to begin, even desired it greatly.
So that, at the first words, no one asked himself for instance where the voice came from.
Surrounded by an extraordinary number of shadows, we heard: "All of you, who are present in my spirit."

IV

They tell that the Prince of Condé slept soundly the night before the battle. Does it seem an unimportant detail?
I don't want to say one thing in place of another, but let the friend of bees take care, for his is a dangerous love.
It's not the first time that an admirable series of causes produces a totally different effect.
In the very same way, at the Inn of the Angels, the beginning was as they tell it and as for what followed it would be clear in the end.
At the time it seemed only an ambiguous sign, a small speck on the horizon.

V

The fact is there wasn't even a child playing on the beach when the storm-front broke away from the farthest horizon and began to advance rapidly.
First, running on the water's edge, it lifted two heavy wings and it hides silently behind cloudbanks; suddenly projecting a light, like that of a comet, it comes toward us.
Then it is too late to put off explanations to another time.
I watch a mystical crumbling of castles in the air.

(RF)

Giulia Niccolai

from SUBSTITUTION

3

From outside the adequate motive,
the suddenly necessary appearance.
From time to time, objects and events,
the indispensable need, the sharing
of convergence.
From the initial impulse, from the constant
sedimentation.
Avoiding changes, contributions, suppressions.
Then it seems clear.
And there you can see yourself
exactly as you are.

5

Shaped by form,
replete with habit,
a possibility opens
and invites to a close connection
reduced to manageable proportions
by an inevitable adaptation:
forewarning and inertia
joined by a common weave.

9

The capacity for contradictions,
the habit quickly smothered
and the crossing-point,
the change.
The choice of these final encounters:
freeing the course
and the particular open
procedure.

(RF & BS)

SUBSTITUTION

For the loss of the center substitute
the destruction of the center
for the loss of a meaning
the negation of a meaning.

You can identify it by the degree
to which it is invincible:
measure all its distance
everywhere (and nowhere).

Thus
the reversibility of the sign
the evanescence of the meaning
the opposite of the senseless

a multiplication of senselessness
an artfully invented farce.

(RF & BS)

POSITIVE & NEGATIVE

Anything can happen
have a meaning or not.

It has no truth to propose
it keeps the meaning open
the sense springs from naming things.

The numbering of a page
a communication of forms
the hypothesis of a reality in motion:
a giddiness of an endless variety
of inversions.

And what you oppose to them
can always be overturned
to its exact opposite.

(RF & BS)

Stanislao Nievo

A HUNDRED-YEAR ABYSS

The currents have passed
gentle waves
for the one who has nothing
beyond the wait

rotting planks
have fallen into the mud
with the fingernails of the dead
in their final scratching

the fish have kissed
the faces of the drowned
swollen with murderous water
beside the iron coffin

for a forgotten secret
an immense wooden wheel
slices the darkness
that has kept it entangled

(IN)

DIALOGUE WITH A MAN DROWNED LONG AGO

Why do you look for me
moved by an opaque piece of wood
destroyed by time?
I kept silent

anxious for them
whose youth is frozen
within the cold nightmare

Under this curved board
whatever stands above thickens
Your gentleness
is of no use

Do you want to dry up with the water
the pain of never having lived?
We died sleeping through the storm
near the most beautiful island in the world

by a flash of lightning
We were forty and the oldest one
was just your age
One of us isn't there

the others are bewitched
by that moment
and they know everything about you
neither wanting to nor loving you

as if chanting for you
the dirge of certain numbers

(IN)

THE CONVERSATION

The face was still
as the midnight sun
its words
were born inside me

is it noble to cry?
or can you only do it in poetic grimaces?
It smiled at distant sounds
and shifted its eyes

the ship
that had dragged him
lacerated to the bottom
returned that day

on the wrong side of fortune

It was raining on the wretched water
and into the foul vapor
the sea crushed
desire locked in the hold

in the colors of woman and of May
Did you die of drowned breath
what remained?
A scruple of nostalgia

that sickens you with sad pleasure
and with the horrible sigh
that no longer exists.
Desperate I resurfaced

like a bubble of desire
that barely bends the air
and bursts

(IN)

Rossana Ombres

BELLA AND THE GOLEM

Whoever has a yod in his name
has the sound of future galaxies:
and he was the prophet of a coming world
above all because of that minuscule yod.

He knew the names of the basilisks
that will inhabit the changing hour of transformation
and of the tortuous leviathan
and of the darting leviathan
that will emerge from the trumpets of the deluge of dust
and of all the saurians
evoked by the great crucible
on which will ride the army
of celestial disinfection.

Even the griffins that will swallow grapes of fire
under the pergola, turned red-hot,
he knew how to address with their proper names:
names with which Shemuel will call them
the angel that has a hundred eyes for a hundred different deaths.

Of Metatron too, the most impervious of angels,
he knew all nine names and the variations in sound
according to the light of day
and the darkness of night
the flowing of tides and the direction of winds.

The day he finished
building the golem
he felt a sharp pain in his right shoulder.
He didn't notice
the angry touch of Ariel
envious prince of inventions
and sorcery,
he didn't see that, flashing, his beard

had acquired the white incandescence
of the supreme mastery of alchemy.

So it came to pass that
a terrifying golem
rose and scoured the panic-stricken streets:
he chose twlight, which more than any hour
resembles falsehood and confusion.
His deformities were those
of an interrupted star left to rot
in the viscid wounds of neglect:
a grim sidereal water corroded him.

The golem carried
in his burrow-maker's hands
golden jewel cases and boxes tied with silk ribbons
so the innocent victims
would not see the instruments of torture;
from a window he took a reverential drape
embroidered with silver pine-cones
and used it as a scarf to conceal
his shoulders' monstrous springe.

"The golem! The golem!" and the spider kicking
with his weed-like legs
broke his web in the center
and jumped in the dark attached to his thread
"The golem! The golem!" and the sea pulled back
the pirate ship stumbled on the sand
and on the stage of its fallen sails
the silver of mullets and barbels
put on a show of sepulchral gymnastics.
"The golem! The golem!" the wild animals
roaming in a painting without perspective
withdrew to the bazels of rings
and the more aggressive ones to the sides of noble portals;
the scaly body of the siren crumbled
revealing that it was
only a prop for museum balconies.
"The golem! The golem!" and the fields poured forth
their crickets and lizards;

a large green seething edema was seen;
the dung-beetle, frightened,
clung to the round coral
of a wet-nurse's necklace.
"The golem! The golem!"

Raziel, who every day encouraged Bella
who was weaving a cape of nettles
locked in the bell tower
(the clock gushed forth its hours
and strokes: so, she, was in no hurry)
took Bella and carried her to where a cave opened
the first in the world
a den still encrusted
with shrimps and original sin.
Bella who has entered the grotto
knows how to read the formula with the right sound
paying attention to the cadence of letters
without making mistakes:
she has a thousand lexical cherubs
inches away from her head,
lika an aureole for saints they go round and round her:
another hundred go from the Name to her eyes
and their every move makes a forest grow.

"The golem! The golem!" shouted a street
that used to sing; and the pigeons, escaping,
composed an indented page . . .
And a storm came
and frogs rained and embers and black stones.

When Bella reads the Name
the golem will be a little pumice ball
but Bella must read it just right
stressing every letter in the appropriate prayer.

The golem is using church domes as shoes!
As gloves he wears twin public buildings!
With his piss he's burned the gardens at the river's edge!
And he doesn't speak!
There: he's near the neighborhood of the merry-go-rounds:
he's turned over the carts of ten sherbet-vendors!

When Bella completes her reading
the Name will fall from the golem.
The golem will explode, leaving only a gray marble
no larger than a juniper berry.
Already, like a soprano, Shemuel is trilling
the frightful song of shattering.

There he is! He collapses! Now he shrinks
and rolls: he ends up in a basin
where pilgrims wash their feet!

Bella has gone back to her cape of nettles.

(EP)

Giorgio Orelli

MARCH STROPHE

A wicked rain with a backhanded
slap.
(My daughter can say what she likes, but tell me something
that begins with an *r* in the middle.)
A woman (pregnant) who hasn't sunbathed in a month
across from my balcony
(I've seen little more than the tips — nothing to boast about —
of her toes).
The wicked rain stops and starts.

But then it stops, and the sun comes back
as in the *Gerusalemme Liberata,*
and the blackbird gives less of a damn than ever
about our chatter, and even the dung, which sparkles squirting
on the fields in broken swarms from the spreader, and these
children who watch each other eat
candy, and
the boy who whistles without knowing it, in defiance of the *cogito.*

(LV)

SECOND TV PROGRAM (or Conflicting Program)

Around ten o'clock
in the sleepy clearing at the top of the palace
the creamy milk rims the ankles
of the National Commission's members,
the Chairman wanders about
(he frequently confuses *blagues* with *bêtises*),
but the three women who sit about my heart
given a little encouragement: "What does he want?,"

says one, very gentle, blonde, "My boss
is a school teacher, a colonel, he's a stickler for commas,
he doesn't know that it's not always the same, that not even the
    comma
always resembles itself." And the other, the tawny one:
"I can't complain about mine, he's a good man from the south,
    if I'm late
he doesn't yell at me too much."
The third, dark, huge, when she wasn't smiling
prematrimonially
stood like a cloud at night, like a mother
in orbit, waiting.

                                      (LV)

SINOPIE

There's one of them, I think his name is Marzio,
every two or three years he stops me as I go by
slowly, on my bicycle, and asks me from the pavement
whether Dante was married and what was his wife's name.
"Gemma," I say, "Gemma Donati." "Ah yes yes, Gemma,"
he says with his smile, "thanks, excuse me."
                                      Another man,
still older, whom I meet more often, it's always I who say hello
first, and I think: maybe he doesn't remember
that rainy windy night when I went out for medicine
and he helped me with his tools (at that hour!)
to fix a wheel mangled by my umbrella.
A third, almost a hundred, deaf,
usually shouts as soon as he sees me: "Hey, young man," and by
    his gesture you can tell
that, if he could, he'd give me a fatherly slap on the shoulder,
but sometimes he limits himself to smiling at me, or, suddenly
    excited,
he exclaims: "You see! the camelia is always the first to bloom,"
or something else, depending on the season.
                                      I'd like
to talk too about some of the others who are already mere sinopie
(without the fine derision of peach and apple trees)
crossed by century-old cracks.

                                      (LV)

FRAGMENT OF THE IDEAL

My ideal was a maid, she used to say: "Thanks, thanks a lot.
Come back tomorrow at this time," in the dark little room
fragrant with her red hair,
while old childless bosses
slept purple covered with spruce.
She didn't address me with the familiar form, but in her dialect's present indicative
the double sibilants hissed.
Hidden with me behind a rock in the woods
where a stream met with melting snow:
"Oh," she said, "it's almost eleven, I have to get back
to her," meaning the grandmother
of some children careless with their toys
a few steps from us. I said to her: "If I can't stand a woman in
        the world . . ."
and "But you know when she gets on her high horse . . . ,"
then I begged her: "Stay a little longer."
With her thick fingers she undid
her watch band and with no more ado
stole at least half an hour. The happy contest
between the clock's and her hands began,
the descending hand opened, was lost in the first real void,
grabbed.
I was young as that water, and yet the maid
didn't want to address me with the familiar form, I didn't have
        a minute's peace
(she's here, there, too much), until one day
— she was alone, ironing — . . .

(LV)

Elio Pagliarani

from **THE BALLAD OF RUDY**

RUDY EXPLAINS

Rudy uses the broom to explain things
actually it's about taking off a shoe
the man whose socks are torn won't make a good impression. Those
    wise guys Walter Chiari and the Maresca girls
to the prettiest woman on the stage a bouquet of gladioli and a
    sash across the shoulder.
    Summer nights
first dancing then a pizza, after pizza the dash into the sea in the
    light of the phosphorescent
foam, it's less beautiful and without surprizes if the moon is out,
    at the crack of dawn
the most worn out are pacing the streets back and forth holding
    on to words, the healthy are making love
    Tomorrow at the Tourist Café
Beppe Marchionni will tell that mosquitoes and horseflies grazed
    off his rear
while making a Swiss chick in the fields old man Marchionni makes
    the rounds
to spit his chaw what a good boy what a nice boy my Peppino
    but his pecker's costing him
over five bucks a day
    evens: through a third party
    These are cries
    from a peasant mother
stifled calls of anxious jealousy for a prep-school son
who hasn't come home yet: she searches the beach with pressure
    in her flushed face
while attendants get the tents set up and rake the sand.

    (JP)

PULLING IN THE SEINE NETS

The job of the sea's hired hands is to pull the nets ashore
on the team the very old have remained, they've always done it
        because at one time there wasn't enough work around
to be choosy and the old men who've only got that work left who
        sleep standing
who eat standing pulling the rope
                        Baiuchela when it's raining lets his
                            wife be next to him
to hold the umbrella while he's barefoot in the sea: sinews tighten in
        the legs
you have to back up waddling in communal rhythm you shift sides,
the rope stretched like elastic one side tied to the harness a dance-
        beat your back
pulls by itself tied by the harness to the rope you eat and you sleep
        at work you dance
a dark dance of slaves tied to the fruit-propitiating rope after the rope
the net where the catch gleams in the bottom
                                he says that each time there's hope
of catching tons of them that's what keeps you at it, that catch that
        night in Classe
that renews delusion without resignation that there's no sense in
        worrying
that the sea's going to dry up
        resignation to the worst is not resignation it's bullying
if you have the awareness of imagining the worst
                there's a dike cutting the current it shifts
sandbars around
        so that when Nandi says throw them out you'd better
                              throw out those nets
right away and turn when he says turn and get down when he says
                        get down and follow a curve
the precise number of feet he tells you to
        there's a hope keeping them hooked
of landing a winter's worth of drunkenness in one try
                        there's actually Nandi's math
that squares things with the moon
        Carlo maintains they get satisfaction

from staring at the net every time it draws near the shore and it's a
                                                           nervous
intermittent light the fish give off jumping inside
                                  but no mind should be paid him
                                  Nandi
the proverbs of the old are a big nothing it's a question of sequences
            the sky and the sea don't matter to him at all
he says and he's been inspecting the sea day and night for a nine mile
            stretch since the eighteen hundreds
without ever forecasting the weather
                                  now that we're drowning in goods
                        and what will Togna say who said you eat it
Lord on high 'cause I'm fed up and tired
                           while throwing in the air a bowl of
                    vegetable soup, what will he say if he's alive
                          in his grave?
I know he's not, be calm, don't smile, but
        he's shouting for sure through my mouth as long as I'm still
                                  hanging on.
Still every night there are men
                    who induce their own sleep
                          by polishing knives that glimmer
they sleep with clenched fists
                awake with bloody impressions of fingernails
                        on the palms of their hands.

                                          (JP)

A DEER IN MASSACHUSETTS

in July
      the little old man has assignments he
forecasts cosmic crises and casts a smiling eye on tables with
wooden cylinders large and small covered by a thin layer of lamp-black
scratched by a long goose quill
                           in Massachusetts
a deer in July
afterwards he points them out with names brushing the wall
the pen-nib of the incline-o-graph lifts off the cylinder he has an
                               older sister he
says we are the puppets of the sun
                            an old man in Massachusetts
who had witnessed the scene from the window of a nearby house
                                  dinner
in Bertinoro with Albana wine in the car at times she gagged
the Doll gagged at times when Rudi hit the brakes on account of the
                               cat lucky that Rudi
has sharp reflexes he held her head in place with his arm
kept her from banging her head on the steering wheel, oh what a
                          laugh he was coming
she swallowed and it went down the wrong way
                            in July in Massachusetts
an old man said that a deer
                   Giorgio now also
wants to be played with when he drives over a hundred
                                sun spots
in Massachusetts? A deer jumped onto
the roof of a three-story house
had a wild look in his eye
staring half an hour at a chasm
that lay below
            sweating is good it cleanses us of humors
we feel refreshed others
catch cold instead what an idiotic dance the *spirù* the deer
jumped off nonchalantly.

                                                        (JP)

Pier Paolo Pasolini

HANDSOME AS A HORSE

My father gave me a hundred lire:
all of twenty, handsome as a horse,
aglow with festivals and joy.

To movies, dances, joy,
to festivals you take the horse;
life, you cost a hundred lire.

I laugh with my hundred lire,
with curls and eyes reddened with joy
and the innocence of a horse.

Gentlemen, I cost you a hundred lire.

(DF)

GRASS FOR RABBITS

I go through the fields of Siest
with my sack on my hard shoulders
among leaves like silver coins and silk.

All the world is silver and silk,
only I am made of tough grasses,
son of a woman of Siest.

They're mean, the peasants of Siest!
If they see me stealing their silk
from the grass, they'll raise their hard hands.

I turn toward the shade of Siest.

(DF)

TESTAMENT

In nineteen forty-four
I worked for the Boté&rs.
Time to us, scorched by
labor's sun, was sacred.
Black clouds on the hearth,
white flecks in the sky
were the fear and the joy
of loving the scythe and the hammer.

I was a youngster of sixteen
with a rough and muddy heart,
eyes like burning roses
and hair like my mother's.
I was beginning to play bocce,
slick my curls, dance on holidays.
Dark shoes!   Light shirts!
Youth, strange earth.

We hunted frogs at night
with lantern and barbed spear.
The canes and grasses bled
under Rico's red lamp
in the bone-freezing dark.
We found fry by the thousands
in the pools of the Sil.
We moved slowly, without a sound.

Dinner done, the entire
company of fellows gathered
in the poplar grove
and there we cursed like demons
and sang like birds.
Then, in the corn shade,
we played some hands of cards.
Mother and father were dead.

On Sundays, men of uncouth heart,
we roved on our bikes

through magic, paragon lands.
And once in the grove's evening
light I saw Neta
taking her sheep to pasture.
With her staff
she moved the silken air.

I smelled of grass and manure
and of sweats resigned
to my hot leather stomach;
and my pants, thrust on
and forgotten since morning,
couldn't conceal desire
swelled with drugged mornings
and nights without freshness of rain.

I tried — the first time —
with that girl of thirteen
and, full of ardor, fled
to tell it to my friends.
It was Saturday, and not even a dog
could be seen in the streets.
Selan's house was on fire.
All the lights were out.

In the middle of the square a corpse
in a pool of frozen blood.
In the town deserted as the sea
four Germans caught me
and cursing madly brought me
to a truck parked in the shade.
Three days later I was hung
from the mulberry by the inn.

I bequeath my image
to the conscience of the rich,
my vacant eyes, my clothes
smelling of my bitter sweats.
I'd no fear of leaving
my youth with the Germans.
Long live the courage, the sorrow
and the innocence of the poor!
(DF)

Camillo Pennati

IMPRISONMENT

I try not to watch the clock on the wall
and surprise time's changing light
as it shifts hour to hour — air
belabors the stone facade beyond my window
caressing the reflection that one stone
mirrors in another while the sky colors them
from above so that I can't see how it changes up there
or how it suffers imperceptible passages
fading into a halo as a wave elsewhere on the water-edge
breathing a different rhythm wipes away
its warp — it presses against me
until it turns dark outside and in that darkening
blooms into a double and my table and lamp
shadow that breathes its impalpable nature
from all solid things. Passing beyond this hour
to another awaited even more anxiously
than imprisonment of my mind meant through love
to interfere with the other
the desire that makes it suffer
though my breathing is still not freed
into that language.

(WSDP)

LEMONS

They swing the ripened heaviness
of their lives in yellow globes
hanging from branches as soon as they take on
the joy of wearily following that overhead weight
to rebalance it so that they arch over
until they open into a wide vortex
of leaves soaring in counterweight

to keep it afloat in mid-air
— each one a radiating concentration —
as from a green mooring absorbing
its shared dizziness and the rebound
in the balance that feels no dismay
as it recognizes itself in the finished half
of each overhanging suspension without revealing where
it will end growing so very slowly and
while leaning thus turns them upside down
in their lemony forms.

They swing
for an instant the weight of a life observing them
hanging in the painful dizziness
shunting them into abstract sympathy
— they swing inside the mind
   and that abyss tries to separate it
   in carefully constructed order from what it feels is missing
   when it would overflow
   that deep desire for dizziness
   till it pulls it back to earth again
   in the root of the world inside the consistency
   of destiny inside the breath of gods
   where eros once infused infuses itself in every likeness
   undoing every network of comfort
   every refuge of vicarious goodness
   in the humbling repression of mind —
but already it reflowers in desperate twisting
in a tangle in which it knows only to bite itself again
in that sheltering landscape which the savage
profusion (the exploding of fear
the terror of transgressing in its jungle image
and likeness where it can lose itself
beyond the concentration camp) immediately buries in sand
during the hard times cancelled by that desert
and disperses it among the years stunned
as if awakening from the very shadow
of that feeling that doesn't exist
nor does the deafened awe of instinct
perceive it.

                                            (WSDP)

THE HOUR SLIDES

It's trying to snow, though winter's greenery
still vibrant in a few bushes defeats the brown
almost black earth where it unwinds
and dissolves, the frisking of a blackbird
ruffled by gusts of wind
while it bends over and pecks.
The smooth sky, like a looming heath
monotonously vast in a whiteness that shines
over there in the angular twining of branches
in black carcasses of bark
beneath which sap begins again to run
through the fable of the skeleton that would weave once more
the green mantle of resurrection.
The light shifts once, twice,
the wind drops as if leaving a footprint
heavier than itself. In the night
the hour slides toward bottom, slowly
like a stagnant pool breaking up.

(WSDP)

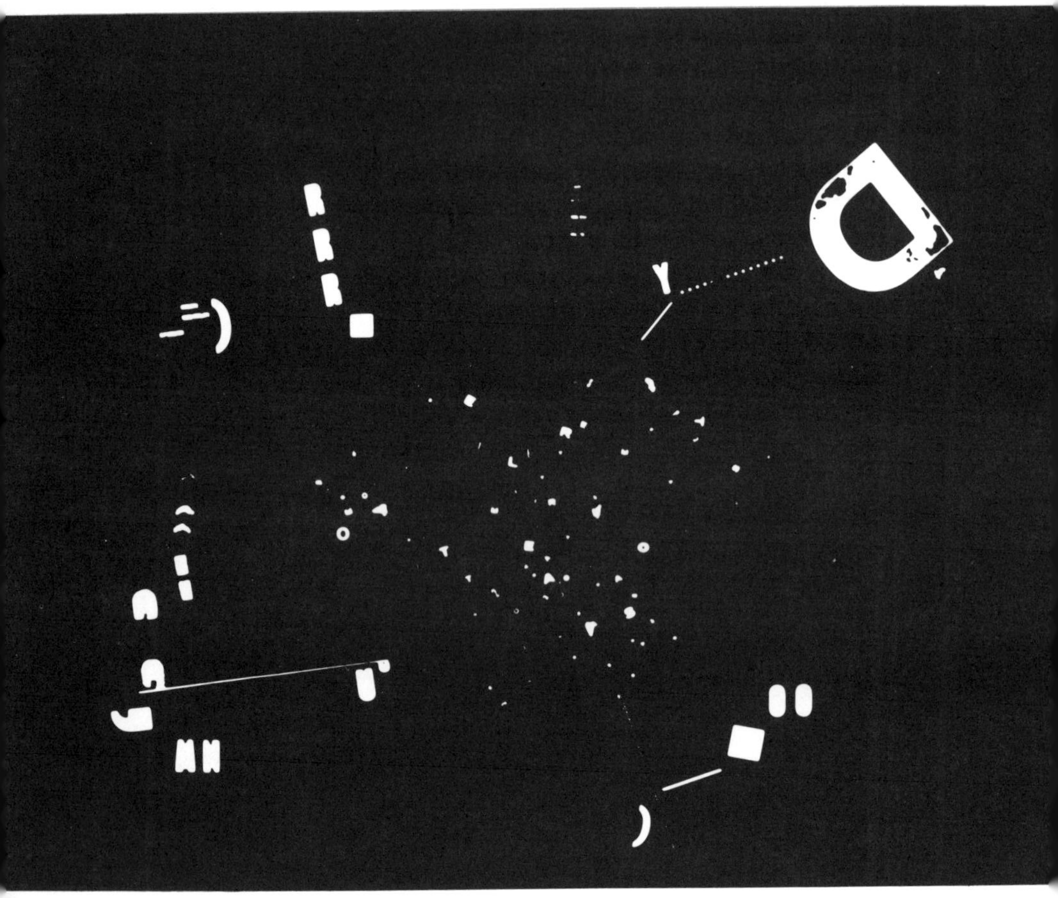

Allessandro Peregalli

THE METAMORPHOSIS

The other day I went to the office
with ass's ears and a lion's deep voice;
at the roar that vibrated like a bray
from my capacious throat (I have thirty-two
teeth in one inner and one outer set and a mouth
that runs all the way to my ears),
everything seemed paralyzed; clerks and supervisors
looked at me with bulging eyes, stupefied;
I made four feline leaps around the room
and they climbed on their desks, howling.
I remember Signor Lentini perched
on top of his desk with a red
swollen face, one leg in the air, his coat
flung up over his shoulders like a flag.
And I remember Signor y Hora making little jumps,
small as he is, threaded into an old suit, his eyes blind
with anger and fear, shouting: "I'm a genius, I'm a genius,
and you forgot that I'm infallible: that's an ass
with a lion's deep voice." And Signor Lentini answered: "No, it's a lion
with ass's ears! Don't you see its feline strength?"
His voice, full of fiery emotion, was muffled in his windpipe
and he had the well-featured face
of a bureaucrat idealist whose real life is
far from everyday affairs. In the meantime, a deep noise
kept gurgling from my lion's throat.
And Signor Archeologo, taking advantage of a table joined to his desk
(in a space consequently much bigger than that conceded to the others)
was giving vent to his Italian temperament in graceful but grotesque
                                                          contortions
hiding his fear under the aegis of four foreign citizenships,
forgetting that he was speaking to a feline animal with ass's ears,
a beast he could not logically have understood anyway.
As for the others, the young ones with their simple sporting souls,
some were playing soccer, some were riding bicycles
in tight whirling turns grazing the edges of desks,

or else they were boxing, transported to the outer limits of their
                                    psychic potentials
by the remarkable adventure they were living through, freeing them
                                from their servitude.
Suddenly, I threw off my mask, lowered my ears to a normal level,
made my mouth more human, no longer like a wild beast, hid my
                                canine teeth
under the placid lip nature had given me,
smiled, standing up straight, and said: "It's me,"
in a normal voice, though I could still hear
the hoarse undertone of my earlier deep gurgle.
And everyone cheered me a lot and wanted to propose me for
                                District Attorney
but I convinced them that wouldn't be appropriate
and that anyway my dignity wouldn't allow me to accept.
Then they spoke a little while longer about this great adventure:
they asked me about transformations,
begged me to repeat the lion's roar and to extend my ears,
all of which I did, pleasing them immensely,
and they ended by enthuiastically praising my cultural skills
and by giving me, as a result, a long letter to type.

                                                                         (DL)

THE DEPARTURE

And now home, home! Wind comes in through the window
like a hero's march; the ringing bell
is like a thousand trumpets bundled
into one single shining sound
and on my desk cascade some names:
Michelangelo, Joyce, Dante, Stravinsky,
weakened by long periods of paid employment.
And the windstorm of our departure, beginning
with a great trampling of feet through the halls,
is like: the sea! the sea! reached

after twenty years of land, is like astonishment
at the sight of a shooting star
miraculous in a leaden cloudy sky; and I think
of imperial battles as I set off awed
by the lethargy of centuries and the sudden
engagement of everything in an instant, lighting
dreams, passions, sentiments, arguments,
memories, actions, images, all there
in a mute and solemn instant of splendor,
as remarkable as an endless
slow-motion explosion or the secret
of universal energy; in this deep surging
overflow I move toward the door,
everyone saying goodbye at the same time;
everyone chorusing goodbye
to our brave leader!
And now home, home! Outside, swept along
by the current of the halls, by the bottle-green
whirlpools of the stairs (the elevator
descending through them in marked stages
like Picard's bathysphere: six thousand
meters under water in supple
multicolored female fauna) outside, under the arch
of the main door which now as I turn back looks like an ogre's cave,
among a thousand little whirlpools of goodbyes, the first glimmer
of open air, sun, daylight, a patch of sky, and still
the echoing goodbyes; in front of me the wall of San Fedele
rises suddenly and harmoniously across the street
and, turning left and waving a last goodbye
to the others and thinking finally I will see my wife again
and enjoy a hearty lunch, I set off
under a brilliant sky with a huge appetite and long and happy strides
on a sea colored by the enormous victory of summer.

(DL)

Danilo Plateo

BE GREEDY

Be greedy
eat the fish that was caught
and the fisherman with the whole line
crush gluttonous patience
and devour yourselves, the State,
the mouth, and this signed page.

I licked my whiskers
like an Andalusian mouse
wringling his snout
at stale scraps
of gorgonzola;
your beam too
was blinded that May
a little Big Cheese

Ah! The bartering of thirteen houses,
some skinny cows
for a metropolis of love.
Gold and brass
heart and goose liver,
(womanish witchcraft)
big shoes and brain too;
oh, I know your mule road
(me, mommy and you
and underwear hanging in the window). I'm leaving!!!!!
A Cadillac
needs superhighways.

Between the flourishes and the roar
of the small mechanical mole
here is Centocelle, prism of pure clay.
In the corner of one of many "workers' " bars,
one two three black shiny splotches
written on the crumbling plaster wall mock me

with "Kilroy was here!"
Dear small buddhas, static in
their energy.
Seeing them from afar (I think)
they would seem: one at the market, another at the pool hall,
others at demonstrations
a people of industrious anarchistic ants.

Mimosa I'll bring you
I'll bring you mimosa
Hooligan — Revolution + Drum.
And wine and bread
(don't reject the flower-decked chef 5 times)
the sixth time he'll kiss you on the mouth.

Woman, I have sculpted you,
made of you a hammer and an awl
when the work was done I struck you
"Why don't you speak ingrate, wretch?"
And you? You dared what Moses feared
I forgave you seventy times seven
but a feminist no, marble has two tits.

(RAM)

Antonio Porta

ANIMAL, VEGETABLE

That deer, its wary brow having pierced the surroundings,
took off bounding in great circles
over the vast meadow: in flight it snatched at
the long grasses all around until the hemlock grass
turned it to stone. The tree spread its skeleton
searching for space among the trees; with its plumed tip
it soon surpassed the forest's height by a hand's breadth:
two foresters marked it with a brand,
to signal the point of attack to the axe.
The yellow insect crawled along the tree
to dangle from high leaves broad as lakes.
The break of Bucorvo red and curved like an
ivory bridge intervened
to spatter its back. That flower, leaves and petals spread
to improbable widths; hummingbirds and thick flocks
of insects managed to light there.
Bungler and dolt, the explorer, chopping it down,
with violent fingers, brutalized it.
That rat sharpened its needle eyes staring at a swift cloud
that swelled as it climbed,
exploded, violent plumes whistling in the air:
left exposed, desert rat, it was torn to pieces
by the watchful falcon. The bird forgot
the bushes' thickness, sucked a long worm
from the clods: two urchin friends,
on the watch managed to pierce
its throat, nailing its prey
half in half out of the beak.

(RF&BS)

OPENING

1

Behind the door nothing, behind the curtain,
the imprint pressed on the wall, underneath,
the car, the window, it stops, behind the curtain,
a wind shaking it, on the black ceiling
a darker stain, imprint of the hand
rising he leaned, nothing, pressing,
a silk handkerchief, the chandelier sways,
a knot, the light, ink-spot,
on the floor, above the curtain, the straw hat rasping,
on the floor drops of sweat, rising,
the stain doesn't disappear, behind the curtain,
the black silk of the handkerchief, gleams on the ceiling,
the hand rests, the fire in the hand,
on the armchair a silk knot, it shimmers,
the wound, now the blood on the ceiling,
the handkerchief silk waves a hand.

2

She slips on stockings, peels them off with her teeth,
the splits, the double somersault, in an instant, the leotard,
backwards, somersault, then the splits, breasts
press against the floor, behind the hair, behind the door,
there isn't, there is the backward leap, the seams,
the hand-print, reversed, on the ceiling,
the cartwheel, of legs and arms, sideways,
of breasts, the eyes, white, against the ceiling,
behind the door, silk stockings hanging, the somersault.

3

Because the curtain shakes, it has risen,
the wind, in the gap the light, the dark,
behind the curtain there is night, day,
in the canals barges, in a group, the quiet canals,
they sail, loaded with sand, under the bridges,

it's morning, the iron of footsteps, oars and motors,
footsteps on the sand, wind on the sand,
the curtains lift their edges, because it's night,
day of wind, of rain on the sea,
behind the door the sea, the curtain fills with sand,
with stockings, rain, hanging, soiled with blood.

4

The point, the high window, there was wind,
it rose slowly, shrieks, in an instant,
oval, a hole in the wall, with the hand,
in splinters, the oval of the glass, on the leaves,
it's night, morning, thick, dense, clear,
of sand, of diamond, it runs on the beach,
risen and raced, the hand pushed, at length,
firm against the glass, the brow, on the,
the glass on the morning, presses, dark,
the hand sinks, into the earth, onto the glass, into the belly,
the glass brow, sand clouds,
in the tent, ripped belly, behind the door.

5

Cartwheel of legs, the canvas flaps in the wind,
that man, legs stick to the race,
the rope sags, toward the jetty, on the sand,
above the nets, they dry, the sneakers,
the cement jetty, they beat the race,
there is only sea, always darker, cement,
in the tent, she peeled off her stockings with her teeth,
the point, she has pressed it an instant, at length,
the stockings spread out on the water, on the belly.

6

Over there, she grasps the handle, toward,
there is not, neither certainty, nor exit, on the wall,
the ear, then opening, uncertain, it doesn't open,
a reply, keys between fingers, the belly open,

the hand on the belly, it trembles on the leaves,
runnning, on the sand, point of the blade,
the son, under the desk, sleeps in the room.

7

The body on the cliff, the blind eye, sun,
wall, he was sleeping, head on book, night on sea,
behind the window birds, sun in the tent,
the darker eye, slash in the belly, under the imprint,
behind the tent, the end, opening, in the wall,
a hole, dried-up belly, the closed door,
the door opens, closes, belly pressed,
that opens, wall, night, door.

(RF&BS)

Vasco Pratolini

from **1967 CALENDAR**

JANUARY

Florence after the flood.
. . . .
. . . .

The marking of the diesel oil touches
the (magical) railing on Magazzini Street.

Do you understand now what divides us?
You have turned to me nimbly:
*"Le jeune homme dont l'oeil est brillant; la peau brune
Le beau corps de vingt ans . . ."*

Your loving mockery
the ancient books you must rescue
your broken nails, benumbed breasts
your youth armed only with future.

MARCH

as if

I have written about you only once,
never in books where somebody thought he recognized you
as if each father figure were K.'s father
to whom only one letter is addressed and who can turn
into a symbol but like the block
of stone that still intact resembles the Prisoners
whom the chisel will free, chaining them to pain,
listen,
within my limits it represents an offer,
how often I fake to myself I offered you a shred of life

which you, an old man, labored to spell out.
                          That time only
I entitled a chapter of my story "My Father"
and dreamed of how we could have been, you and I,
still close to the truth, as if then not now
I took leave of your face and of our common
past: the woman who was our wife and mother
who passed through your memory oh not because of your bad
conscience but because of the insult time inflicts
if we do not stop it for a second and our blood
no longer uses it as nourishment.
                         Until today
when I have lost my father and it is as if I lost
an old-time friend of whom I was deeply fond.

JUNE

In the days when Israel offends
so that we remember the century-old and the recent
offenses received by her people and it inflicts the extermination
that was inflicted on her on the table of moral
values, Reder, the executioner, pleads for forgiveness
from the Marzabotto victims oh how time
rightly rends, rather than healing the wounds
and we all, the offended and the offenders, are on this
boat hobbling towards a forever future sea,
where between quicksands and peaks of wisdom
the proletarian hemisphere expands.

JULY

Here between Vestro House and Lama House,
the olive trees the cypress trees the mulberry tree the pine
balanced on its roots, meets
the hare with a tuft of grass in its mouth or the fox
that stiffens statue-like when hit by headlights, the frog
the owl the eternal grasshopper the ant the water snake

the family of pheasants in single file,
all as if from another age. . .
    Though the freeway runs parallel
and the latest model tractor climbs the banks
toward homes with no electric power, callous
abuses are perpetuated, "a black and white island in the red
Valdarno" we find solace and relax before
the battery-powered tube, and the motor-drawn water: "great!
great!" but we rush to the car so that in its newspapers
Arezzo may tell us of blacks rioting on Fifth Avenue
of Vietnam Bolivia Angola . . .
    When we return for a long moment the hail
mantles fields and homes spreading
desolation: "oh the crops, the broken vines,
the shaken olive trees, the ruined vegetables," we talk to
the old communist field hand about the metalworkers'
strike at the Alfa-Sud plant and Togliatti
"may he rest in peace" he states with conviction.
    After the hail
the fog rolls down from Pratomagno and we remain
up here removed from heaven and earth.

DECEMBER

There is no balance,
a year like today here in Turin
the frost bites at your fingers.
Mirafiori boils with a fury that now
knows its own reasons well and masters them.
                        Yesterday the dead dog
at the foot of the great pine tree was a watchful
presence over Lama House where we drank toasts
with old friends.
                      There is only expectation.
And the certainty that tomorrow will not be another day like many
                                                others.

                                        (GC&KDA)

Giovanni Raboni

[Untitled]

"An Auschwitz doctor" he seemed to us
the first time. At the end (visits, negotiations
and the rest) a good lame devil. Looking at each other with a smile
of people who would rather not be there or vomiting
was our business after all, the terrain
neutral, elevator cage
or landing. Beyond the door was his business. Beyond the door
is entirely his business, beginning
with the sudden scruples I couldn't manage to feel. "In all good con-
science
I advise against it – no, it's not more difficult, it's something
different: in the first month it's all right: there's a kind
of baby now, to destroy." Was he looking at his glass cabinet
while talking or was
somebody else? Yes, too bad, I wanted
to tell him, too bad, don't think about it, be brave.

Glass cabinet of seaweed. Of
dwarf trees. In sleep, summed up, that bit
of city green.
Superficially in sleep our story fragments.
In the Park, I was saying, there are monsters; in the Public Garden,
soldiers.
Not so neutral really – a cage that climbs
very slowly inside blocks of light. Nothing was hard, there was
a parking-space in front of the door,
rubbish stacked neatly in the courtyard. In the silence
that shrivels our stomachs (and: idiot, I was thinking,
idiot, animal, how did you get into this fix again??)
there must be something somewhere
to eat, sluggish four-footed
animal, confused plural person...

(RF&BS)

ECONOMICS OF FEAR

They can. They always can. And without any warning. And without? They don't come and tell you first, that's for sure. However, you understood that. Yes, I think I understood it. A click. I knew that one notices. A tape? Of course, a tape; what did you expect? Gnomes. Caves for listening. Mazes of cork. No way. A tape. And afterwards? They throw away ninety percent of them. They don't do it in time. Probably it doesn't interest him. Not at my level. And then? A case. They had explained it to me. However, listen, we're even. As always. I didn't know it either. Not this, the other thing. But leaving aside the not knowing. A kind of compensation. Of symmetry. No, naturally I knew perfectly well what effect it has. I didn't know they used it for general anesthesia. As coadjutant. I didn't know they used it as coadjutant in general anesthesia. Still, are you sure we're doing the right thing? If you're sure it's there, wouldn't it be a good idea to talk as though it weren't? Eh. Eh what? Is it really a good idea to talk? But of course, what do you think, that they have it in for the two of us? Not even for me, in all probability, certainly not for me. But I don't say it's them. Who are they? I don't know, but in any case not them, I was thinking of just anyone at all. They can't run risks of this kind. Funny, now it's they who are running risks. I said they can't run them. To tell you the truth, I thought if it was anyone it was you. You're crazy. Well why, then? By chance. A kind of tic. Or like those molecules. You remember organic chemistry? Neither do I. Listen, I'm afraid. But if I told you they have nothing against me. No, the other thing. Suppose he's there when I'm waking up. That's when you talk. But it will be a minimal dose, no? As coadjutant. Enough to make you talk. I know you talk. They told me so. I know.

2.

I don't know how many days it's been. They don't come and tell you first, that's for sure. I don't remember when I heard the click. Not many days ago. I knew that one notices. They had explained it to me. The tape begins to revolve. They throw away ninety per cent. They don't do it in time, I think. They can't listen to them all. They keep them for a little while before throwing them away. Unless they really are of interest to someone. But me, imagine. So much the less the two of us. Chance. A kind of tic. Or a molecular structure, or something of the sort. I couldn't say just what. I don't remember ... Anyhow we're even. As always. In a certain sense. A certain symmetry. A kind of compensation. Me with this remote leech, and you. Just think: I didn't know. I was aware of the specific use, naturally. I mean, intentional. The effect pursued intentionally. However, it doesn't seem to me that's the case here. A minimal dose, no? As coadjutant. There's no reason to be afraid. It will be OK if he's not there when you're waking up. But even if he is. Don't call me by name. Not when we're making love. I don't remember. I don't think so.

3.

I didn't know it was possible. I thought it wasn't possible. That a paper was needed. Like for searches. Maybe it's better if I don't phone you for a while. It bothers me to think there's someone listening in. I picture myself as a kind of gnome. In a cave. Cork walls full of suckers. But even if there is a tape-recorder. I talk and remain there. On the tape. It makes sense to me. It may end up in someone's hands. Anyone's at all. They keep them for a little while before throwing them away. Listen, I'm afraid. No, of the other thing. Even you didn't know about that. We're even. They use it as anesthesia. As coadjutant. A big enough dose to make you talk. Suppose he's there when I'm waking up.

(RF)

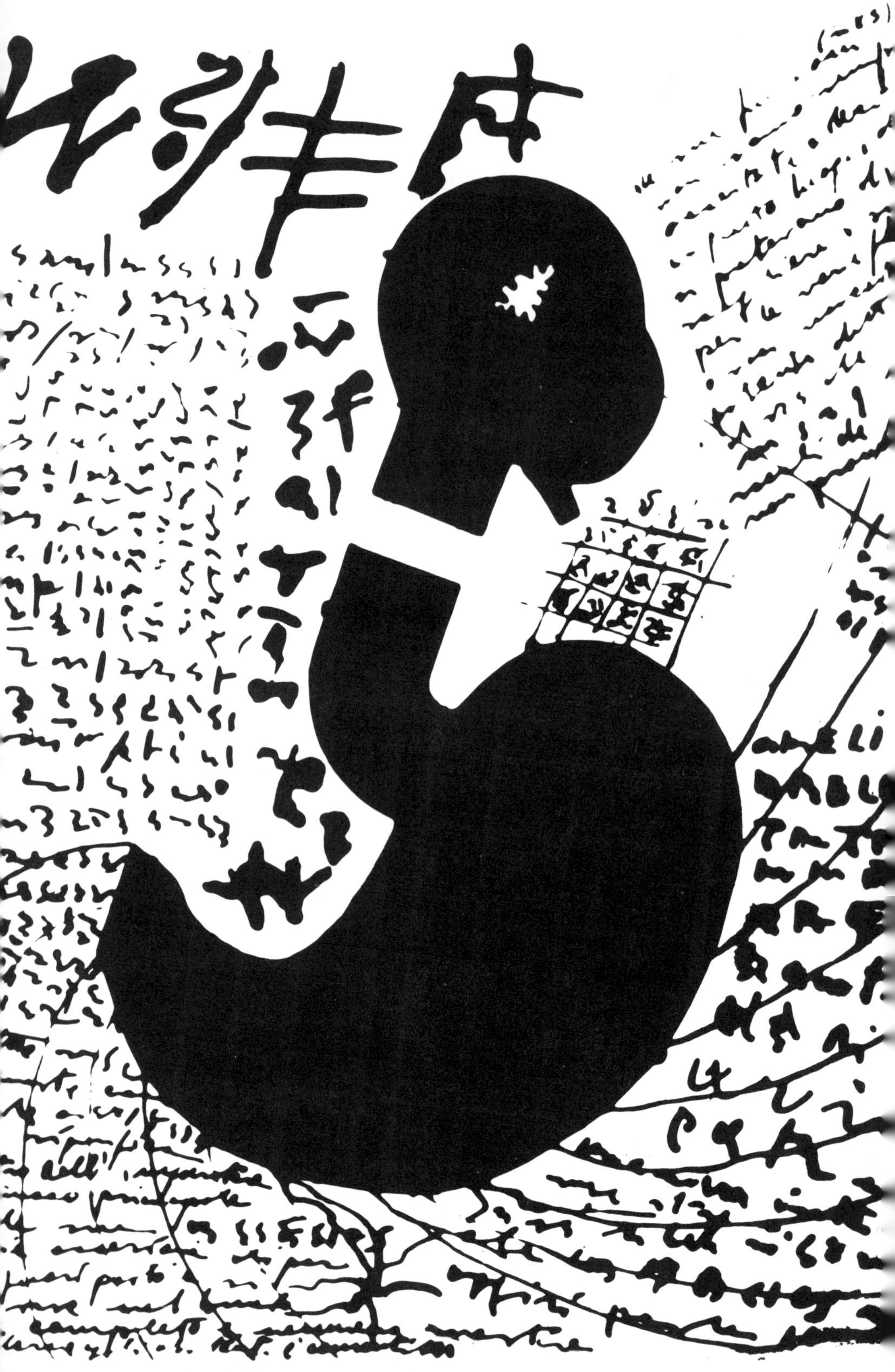

Silvio Ramat

CRUISE

Between a quick phone call and love at first sight
your hasty decisions;   the train wobbles,
a toy gone off the rails: you are defrosting
from inside the glass.   You don't arrive: you're leaving.
The line is all yours: you leave us
more and less than an address, two dates
somewhat too precise, the dry cut
of timetables.   But in between
whirls the most chaotic diary
of excursions, other departures other returns,
comings and goings in the fixity
of oceans that mirror you, of skies that don't age you.

Between given extremes — still time and space —
is everything optional?   Think that we think you
free as the absurd in the necessity
of a huge cage blooming with steel,
prisoner who go around reassuring yourself
of how greatly dense walls limit
your hopes of flight.   Space
you live: it's that deep
suspension of time, while those you leave behind
suffer the loss of time's expansion,
count the minute grains of minutes
that you can already scatter meanwhile
in tufts of cloud, in azure foam.

Does the news that precedes you into port
still sing this death of time for you,
or does it sing the time of our death?

(AB)

STAGE DIRECTIONS FOR FUTURE SILENCES

(1)

Failures without ecstasy to make up for them
vex the plot of the age:
recoverable?   recovered,
and already memory, alive at the border.
My prehistory doesn't cover me, at the final
gap I ready myself: I am I
here, too, where I drown with eyes open.

(2)

You will fail;   but will the abyss be an ecstasy?
Think what thick ages of plots
I'd relive, and what a series of traumas,
between the active margins of remembrance
My shyness and yours make the final
gap: and you, white guardian angel — hold me
again, to fill it up with eyes open.

(3)

My deceit, my total servitude,
I learn by what plots you regenerate.
I recover myself if I blind myself,
excited by the sun of remembrance.
The mirror of tenderness is the final
gap.   Will I manage, short of ecstasy,
to say it, to navigate it with eyes open?

(AB)

FEAST OF THE GODS

He who is able to play with fire
will soon kiss the wind,
will dine with water and sun,
will want to feed on them — communing
with the creatures of the Canticle: all of them,
not excluding sister death
nor the moon. But a moon that doesn't sing:
maybe she prays while she sleeps,   the sumptuous
guest —or not? — at the feast, that hardens
into inseparable crumbs, flavorless prisms,
or curdles into stiff rafia
dahlias, into dead chalk peaches
pecked by motionless cardboard birds
that, in profile, seem weightless for flight:
this uncontainable lunar leap
that already brings them home to Olympus.

(AB)

Franco Rella

FOUR MOVEMENTS FOR VOICES

I. (for C. and G.S.)

and in the tangle moist tide breaks returns
in the hieroglyph singing voices and letters
a crack climbs and there gold motes

an order a square a crystal
the usual deceit tide or a cloud or voices
or gestures or bodies silently touching

letters and bodies cross and loud voices and a
crystal or square a sign breaks in the
tangle a thing returns again a story

II.

and in the tangle of signs or of gestures or sounds
a thing or a body a sign an order or a
space a place a way a road a story

an event or a wait in the tangle waiting
they silently intertwine and a trace returns in the
journey a sign breaks a series a sound

smoothly evenly it breaks again it opens in the
middle while an event fulfills itself oh these
voices oh the silence they sing oh these signs

III.

a clue a trace in this inert place
or a crack precipitating a knot of
misdeeds a tangle that doesn't seem a whirl

a mask of deeds or of voices a series

of silent organs or in the silence or the streets
or bodies or wisdom or an enigma or still

a story or order or a square a crystal
a hieroglyph a tangle or signs which
silently intertwine here now celebrating gently wait

        IV. (summary)

celebrating gently wait or a story or
stories (or a story within stories) or still
searching (in the tangle) for a deception (or still:
a negation, presumed)
              oh the immense wisdom
Oedipus and the Sphinx, precipitating
                    a tangle of
misdeeds
    a crime: investigating, the reason or
the cause, but these singing voices but these
laughing voices but these strident voices, celebrating
the wait
    asking, but running through these streets,
but an order, or a crystal, or a square, or a
series
    and wind and dust and this window and
the streets and running through these streets and a gap
a crack, and a struggle (and the description: of a
battle), the reason and the cause, a contradiction,
a negation
        (and a story, then, or
the story)
    in this place, in this space
now, then.

                        (RAM)

Nelo Risi

[Untitled]

Armaments have a life of their own—
the photograph of four pairs of camels
towing a crippled tank across the sand
against a green and fiery sunset
dates from yesterday
I found out then it was a Sherman
that had seen service at Naples and Cassino
and the NATO manoeuvres in Sardinia
later demoted to the level of the piazza
just to oppose the populace
then sold for its scrap value
to a dealer in Pavia who unloaded it
on Nasser as new
It had its new Pirelli tracks
and a lighter Breda turret
It was last seen at Gaza
legs upended in the desert its dome
blown off like a pot lid
Curiously the compass on board
had remained intact
and was promptly resold
by a blue-helmeted UN soldier to a friend
who was leaving as a mercenary for Katanga
where today by way of an ambush
it decorates the neck of a black sergeant
who . . .
                         (RF&BS)

A TRULY WORLDWIDE SERVICE

: — The only industry in a position to offer you
explosive novelties / Visit us!
and the peddler upright among flags and missiles
with the arch of peace at his back
with a cobalt-blue flash in his eyes

and a radar dance in his ears
fires a shot
just to keep the Piazza on its toes
                                      — Housewives!
where the bomb lands even the dirt departs
Consumers! a thousand-year-old industry
entirely at your
                service at prewar
prices and on the installment plan
                            on request
delivered in all countries
                over
(including Switzerland) and underdeveloped!
Quality merchandise
                    anyone who tries it
                                    is left breathless!
Jesubambino makes his way forward
through the crowd
does his clever cybernetic exercises
slips all the way down a mortar's mouth
jumps on a mine
tosses a gadget into the pond (oh!
the fish that float to the surface
in the gardens of childhood)
leaves by jet
frightens a dove *(qui ouvre*
                    son bec
and drops the olive-branch)
manoeuvres a white Red Cross train
that derails
       then wants
but all for himself a beautiful
battleship with planes and rockets

The peddler wraps it for him
throwing in a Bic
for free
       The crowd
under the platform disperses

while the voice goes on unsubdued
                              — Special!
because of the holidays! for those
                              and they are legion
who buy at least
              a thousand
tanks or two million machine-guns / a magnificent lottery
     with five free trips / only for families of the mutilated
     / to one of our overseas bases . . .

                                        (RF&BS)

Roberto Roversi

POLITICAL CUSTOMS

I

How old were you when the Medes broke through?

II

The oath by candlelight
in Brunswick Cathedral
before the tomb
of Henry the Fowler (see page 80)
with blue eyes and blond hair, that
and hair on his heart . . .

III

There's no road.   There is a road (a river), there's a river
—I believe there is, it's so—a deep
ditch, a hedge, a tree blossom
under the soggy sou'wester, there are the tears
of a naked baby with trachoma there is
the blood of a decapitated man on the ground
the milt of an animal on the wooden pen;
there is the white thread (a red thread) which extends
from the lips of him who speaks to a house over there,
a map on which the finger creeps in terror,
the woman's orgasm in the grass burned
by an old fire, a bombardier you don't see.
Scorn of institutions (of grave but lawful crimes).
There is no longer an echo, there is no sound, the punches
of the last dispute, the placated
voices (finally?), the unseemly misprints,
another pot of lead boils for more worthy poems
—the characteristic of the times is a cautious indifference,
everything is a little bit interesting for a little while,
everything dies, decays, burns itself out and scatters
in the furnace of memory.

IV

Kant says that the discipline of genius
(i.e. education) is taste: it notches
its wings and makes it clean and well-mannered.
The great Kant, wise in his wooden
garret, with the wave of ideas
which dissolve into an ordered silence
and on the streets (deserted) the horse's hoof.
But he, sitting on his bottom too, is a man, in the house
with moderate heat, on the fifth floor
of an Italian village, what is, what will be? thus distant
from noises. Ah, it isn't fashionable and polished. Not
                                                fashionable,
it's all chipped inside, hanging,
insolent, tender and clear, muscle
butchered in a filthy act of infamy,
miserable obstruction, it is scattered dry weed
gathered by an old hag who sacks it.
This will not be polished, oh no, fashionable it is not (the
                                                circumstances
don't permit it), it is not polished—on the street everyone
hears the hoof of the Angel of Death
passing, alternating his sound with that of the street sweeper
(and his trumpet). The dawn, at dawn, the dawn
—to sketch on the windows with your breath—
it is, in the squeezing of the veins,
so stretched out distant, the open hand, this day's
eye socket uncertain in its choice, it will collapse
among us raving (right away, among us) of ancient woes
and of new devices. It warns us thus reserved proud
not to lose opportunities (life is a thunderbolt in time)
in the meantime—a girl on perfect legs
within the limits of a room puts on the nightgown
plucks herself in the scirocco wounded by a stocking
she laughs at the variety of moods
stirred up by an innocuous hope.

V

To light a cigarette (smoked after 6 years).
Power to the workers and the peasants
—they annul one another overwhelmed
by these contradictions which don't distinguish
between necessity and need, between him who
(one might say) has a rope which unravels
and hangs on to the end and him who, deprived of authority,
                                                            exhausted,
allows the rope to hit him in the face.
The matter is serious and merits consideration.
Subject of every dispute, *in the heat of the room*
while outside one opens up the world
destroyed by the cloudburst
and with the throat of a cow regurgitates a sewer
and night falls in the midst of the lightning
and our piety spreads out over the immobile forms
(including us) in the perfidious suspense of the spectacle
—the perfect mind, usury, the syllogism,
the pun on the title of him who takes his pleasure at the cafe' —
it's
the end of the world, a capsized ark,
the bones of the city on the plains
—then you say that the moment of contrast
justifies itself in a new necessity (this is the point),
every one of us who sits
syllogizes but doesn't work, argument becomes archaic
and all of us (the circling motion of the finger is wide)
lower ourselves in mystification.
To light a cigarette.
Are they dark years or new years?
For in truth I believe that the darkness
is the sullen, dismal, icy, perfect darkness
which is a new light.

VI

Yesterday in Via Andegari dark and narrow, classy street which
                                                                     leads to
a forest of shabby symbols I meet I met I have met the wife
of an executed comrade.
The leaves of memory rustle.
With a head of red hair, in those houses filthy with mud or
with dull bourgeois greed the modulated shoulder played sweetly.
Her youth (enchanted) still.
The time of day, uncertain a bit overflowing
or rather the place detached from remorse, in an uncertain
shadow, detached from the obsessive thunderstorm,
the cheerful happy voice of goodbye so long
or R. who (just a second) . . . forgotten, in my heart . . .
One can forget the dead forever.
With light hearts we went arm in arm
her flaming hair said I am married I have two sons
not even a snapshot anymore, you can understand
my great desire to live
this city drives you crazy.
The country bores you to death.
At night still in her house, among the sons and the husband
in the house suspended in mid-air
on the branches of a happy crystal tree, green.
She kissed me on my perfidious
mouth, and sweetly, at the door.
Everything vanished, drowsy, obliterated, drowned,
faces of dead men who have passed away whiten in the dust
nothing was true anymore.

                                                                                       (LS)

Sergio Salvi

THE KING OF THE WELDERS

He opened his head, with a nutcracker.

He removed, with care, the two immaculate
kernels of his brain, drew
from his pocket a linen handkerchief
embroidered in gold with his initials (Q.Q.),
calmly he wrapped his brain inside, then,
suddenly nervous, turned
all at once,
even sneezed, and threw
the glowing bundle out the window.

Quiet again he got back in line
in the pitch black of the corridor,
the line of the brainless which by now
touched, with the forehead of the first, the door
of the king of the welders,
he who holds,
with charity and firmness,
from the beginning of the ages,
between clouds of sparks and an odorous
tempest of iron filings,
the flame-cutting scepter.

(J.G.)

COUPLE

Who are these two who banter smile
feel their way along the trail
bordered yesterday by red raspberries
bursting in the sun
today
today under the shadow of the viaduct
that crosses the valley in a hissing span
tomorrow
tomorrow surely swallowed by the dark
grass spit up by the earth
(paths are often mortal)
coughed up from the gnawed lungs of the age-old earth
who are these two who nibble the shadows
with their old bodies so graceful in sweaters and slacks
stretched over testicles and breasts
feet covered by callouses and blisters
where swan's wings grow
who are these two who always stumble these two
already well along in years
already well along in their desire
to feel each other's breasts and testicles
without wrinkling their sweaters and slacks
who are these two who sob and moan now
who hurry along the mortal path
who run with hurting feet
in splendid shoes
he with capped teeth and bad eyes
from the diabetes he doesn't know he has had for 1016 days
she with a glass eye bought in a boutique
skillfully concealed between socket and glasses
(but my lord what pointed, flowing breasts
and what heavy testicles)
who are they who are these two tender middle-aged lovers
so healthy and so sick so young and so old
barely emerged from the meshes
of a rest-stop's protective net
barely emerged from the leaves
of a hedge of scrawny oleanders

barely emerged from the lap of the motor-way
a vagina of wisdom an asphalt that has heard
for a long time
pistons jam and spark plugs sputter
leaf springs break and tires blow
even
a couple of old youngsters
get out of a car
and look for night in the daytime . . .

These two are clearly two edges of life retracting
these two are really death united advancing.

(JG)

Giovanna Sandri

from EMPEDOCLES D'ARTAUD

FRAGMENT 57

            from the earth numerous neckless
heads were born
            as if the gods
wished to demonstrate their powers
with these strange signatures

            and there were arms
wandering naked and shoulderless
                  the
right arm stretched out stiff as a bolt
edged by a streak of light
                was not
pointing in a usual direction

a naked man from a large window
                  his
eyes wandering without a forehead
              his head
           a large hole
a sort of circular cavity
             where
in turn   and according
      to the time of day
the sun and moon appeared

                      (RF&BS)

FRAGMENT 61

    (many creatures) were born with faces
and chests oriented
               in different
directions
                     all the rocks were shaped
like a woman's chest
with two breasts perfectly outlined

                    some (creatures)
offspring of human-faced oxen
                         you
could count their ribs
seven to a side
                        others
on the other hand   came into the world
                     offspring
of men with ox heads
                     twice
the same animal head
                and creatures in which
men's and women's natures
were mixed
                  and provided with
sterile parts
         in place of the navel
a brilliant triangle glowed

                       (RF&BS)

AS MUCH AS THEY HIDE

night

aboard

ship

height
of
a star

birds
shining
fallen
from
the clouds

unveiling as much as they hide

(RF&BS)

ONCE IT WAS

thanks to some dark wine
the waves
break
more
gently   look
there's the hoop of
a barrel   once
it was
full
of

(RF&BS)

Roberto Sanesi

JOURNEY TOWARD THE NORTH

Lichen, moss, trolls, arguments
of ancient salt-encrusted casks,
                       and conifers, maybe,
marching upon a granitic pack in the gulf stream, past
the arctic circle of your eyes.
                 And again: gneiss, time overturned,
saltations of the bust, opposition of the head,
the cloud that swells the circumference of the arms
around the solemn face, the nights that lie beneath settling down
with the color of dusk.
            Hypnosis.
                   And the distances
diminish — the foot on the stairs, the door,
her glance.
           The journey has been long. I know.
You have surmounted the burnished walls
of extinction and ecstasy,
        the tombs in the shape of women,
     the tara
of serene green bronze, and you have smothered the cry
of the nimble pollulant uroboros. The roots
and circular flight of the wind have touched
the grain that sprouted already
in your hair.
      I insist.
          You lose yourself in a rose
like a sherpa in an isle. Salt and mould. Butterflies
like shoals of herring quiver through the depths
of your voice.
          And patiently you bind, cultivate
and protect the pollen and ashes.
                A dense perfume
of violet air and organisms in the livid margin
of moraines, crevices, regurgitation of breaths, queries
(and unbroken sounds: "to dare to fall asleep,

the dog between your legs"), and in the smoke
                  — the peat, the waters —
the latitude north at 68 degrees.
                          Down there, where the cold
sometimes stammers at the snow bunting's bony splash
and cuts, for an instant only,
with a feigned springtime the fixed horizon
in the pupils, I ask you,
                 overturning
per aspera ad astrid the lands
where remote gulls pierce with their beaks
a long-shadowed maelstrom,
                     what thing, what words
rip the Lofoton to the reverberation
of your silences?
          The snow
has violet striations, footprints appear, the birds
form low-flying columns with strident notes
along the perfection of the glance, fingers
flutter on the snow.
             Insensibly
shapes like bedspreads of white wolves
beckon you from a wall of clouds,
or crippled enigmatic smiles, on which fear
is put to rest.   Difficult
to awaken all the way to you.

                                              (WA)

THE CUT IN THE ROCK

Light buried in the grain of the rock,
and the cut white with faeces and generations of fish
falls like a blunt shadow, a thing of whitelight
where bracken sway with hard-backed leaves,
noxious herbs, metal and rock in a lone burst of roots
from an overhanging sky. The varying light has no reflections
when you walk with care. Neither gesture nor voice
is in the rain. And so it will be harder to hear
whoever shouts the story from the rainbow.

                                              (WA)

SMALL MOUNTAIN LANDSCAPE

On the summit a drizzle of rusted trees
and the snow,
        my writing scratched in the snow
by a dog's back paws,
           runs through the gorges, artifice,
the deceitful equestrian tricks
of alphabets in the optics of a hawk,
         and a cloud dangles
in the thrilling of the firs.
                Yes, in the spring
this mountain was a fish, it flew,
     unnatural
naturalness of nature that disseminates itself
playing the mad poet's part.

                            (WA)

NORTHWARDS OF THIRTY

Northwards of thirty, beyond greenhouse and fire
of a house not mine high on the hill, and white flowers and crows
climb the shadow, behold, for the first time I speak of myself,
and my words have the sound of panes, that lightly-shattering sound
when blindly birds beat them with their wings, blinded by wind
and drunk in their own cries, and I stay a while in the garden,
I sit, and my words have a lightly-shattering sound.

Sustain, maturity, this effort of intellect and dreams, disdain
the facile hendecasyllable, all the memories, and the person closed
in these affectionate poetic phrases, and let reality beat
like the Atlantic on the cliffs that cross low on the horizon
against a sky where grass and gulls shake the clouds, and be
the essence of each, the contradictions, crow and flower:
the luminous obscurity of words now, again, and always revealed
in this softly climbing shadow of me, seated in the garden.

                            (WA)

Edoardo Sanguineti

PURGATORY OF HELL

1

and they were talking, in the dark (and I, in bed, reading
                    a Sollers novel); and they were talking,
in the hall, and they said, maybe (that is, something like:):
                          but he'll be
delighted (because we're coming in this way, by surprise, in the
                      night, in his room,
in the dark); and they were talking:
    then Anne sat on the easy chair; and Françoise (the second),
and Odile (and Edith), on my bed; and Anne was in her
                      pyjamas; and he woke up
(in his bed); (and said: what do they want?);
    then they brought up the blackboard,
with the idiocies of twisted names (and they read, all together,
aloud);
    then I said to Ollier
that he looked like one of the two priests in *Chien Andalou*;
                      and he
pulled a long face (and said, then: but am I so démodé
                      then?); (and
Chien Andalou is from '29, it seems to me); (and Thibaudeau
shouted: but everything sounds like it's from the novel; mine,
                      that is); (and
Roche said: but we've
got to turn out the lights now);
    and I turned out the lights, and I turned them back on, and
                      then I turned them out again,
one more time; and I said, in the dark, but without moving:
but nothing's happening.

2

beyond that purgatory of gardens (and the white light,
              and the wrought-
iron chairs); and (what's more) beyond the moribund birds
in the greenery:
  there's the Galerie Vivienne;
beyond us, therefore, exists that real graveyard (as I have
         said): three long
boxes of picture postcards, all covered with writing, stamped:
  all to read.

3

just when they were talking: but look at it; (that moon);
         but just then
I was thinking (but tranquil) of the words already written to my
          wife: "but
tranquil"; (having explained): "but tranquil"
        (later): "for-
ever" (that threatening meaning):
  my feet
in the soaking grass, on the path, after the rain, uncertain,
        in the midst of Norman
cows (...); and then the dawn, precisely; and then Madame
       Heurgon, who sees us
from a window of the castle (in the dawn);
  and then it doesn't matter at all, precisely;
(after breakfast, the goodnight, the good morning, in the
       kitchen, in the dawn);
and then: tired of explaining, then, of justifying (of
       justifying myself); (and I
wanted to say, precisely: of justifying myself—as I explained—
        "forever");
  and then:
tired of such insistent returning; (to ghosts); (saying:
       because you will
have noticed how hasty, insistent, I am to go back...;
and so forth); (to ghosts);
  but tranquil, Luciana, really (the 30th
of September), later; but I wish then to say, now: "for-
         ever" (...):

4

so, here (in Cerisy); (so they were saying): we have a Chinese;
(and the Chinese was me, naturally);
    and on the expressway I also explained
the reaction against the literary operation, radically,
                              immediate (and
so forth); and one spoke of triumphant opportunism, even
                        (and when I said, later on,
revisionism, in fact, what I really wanted to say instead
was opportunism);
    because
the Chinese position (I said) justifies every hope (and that
                it might not be a question
of a worker elite, after all, but the end of prehistory,
                              in fact,
and so forth);
    and to my wife I spoke about the quantity of unhappiness,
                          meanwhile (about the
quality and so forth);
    and I wanted to say: it justifies even us; and also our
                                    children;
and I wanted to say: it justifies the moment of utopia (but
                    really, but for us, even,
but here, now): this moment (it justifies);
    and I wanted to say: forever;
(but in the night, in Palermo, I really heard them, the ones
                          who said: why
do you go on living? and they said: how do you justify yourself?
    they said: but do you justify yourself?);
but now, you see: but now, what weariness? and what
                            (in this our
prehistory), what tranquility?
    but you see the mud which sticks on our backs,
and the sun in the trees, and the babies who sleep:
    the babies
who dream (who speak, dreaming); (but the babies, you see
                          them, so restless);
(sleeping, the babies); (dreaming, now):

                                                            (LS)

from **REISEBILDER**

No. 1

what could I say or do, Vasko, when that grave Shirley Temple
came running at me down the Lijnbaan, all technicolor laughter
swishing her red pigtails? I immediately felt her claws —
as they say — dig into my heart:
                                     holding my skull in her
hands though her face is clean now: she sucks on my backbone
up above this desert of Rotterdam, inside this Number One,
here at this literary supper: being (i.e. she) the kind of
thing out of Holbein d.J. (I'm thinking of *Portret van een
onbekende vrouw*): not as well executed, of course, but skinnier:
what with the bat on her head, for example, and without all
that yellow veiling: I asked her name (you heard it too):
something like Inneke, I think:
                             and so what can I write about
now when I still have to carry on until six in the morning
(room 348) with the European Tchicaya and Breyton and you?
                                              (I can't
even phone my wife, you know, or finish *Elective Affinities*): I
even have a few pimples on my face:

No. 8

the one so full of life, sleeping in a corner of the living room:
the one that adores the smooth polished parquet floor: but we
can sense, all of us, that in four months' time it will turn
into something gross:
            we'll bring it back to the woman in slacks
who sold it, at the Café Belvedere, in the sauna courtyard.
this impossible turtle, in a huge Pelikan magic-marker carton
(punches full of holes) with some lettuce leaves (and a slice
of tomato thrown in):
                 this monster that won't communicate:

No. 14

that's us, the couple retreating into the bushes: (their profiles
emerge among the leaves): I lean my arm on your shoulder, my
eyes in yours: and say it really doesn't matter if you haven't
crossed this Jungbrunnen: I say you have no need to:
                                                    but as soon
as you turn your head I become a kind of traffic cop making great
ceremonial gestures on the right-hand edge of the swimming pool
in the midst of a brief flock of Verjungten: see how I'm watched,
now, by that girl running nude toward the spacious Badezelt,
just moments before she disappears inside for good:
                                                    (she's
still the same one, pale and blonde, sitting in front of me,
on the U-Bahn, direction Ruhlenen, Raucher compartment, between
the Ernst-Reuter-Pl. & Theodor-Heuss-Pl. stations, and her ugly
friend with blood-red lips, half-blinded by cigarette smoke,
her glasses propped up in her hair, most likely a student,
tender, with broad open thighs):

                                                    (WSDP)

Francesco Smeraldi

COLOR

My adolescence knew no colors
I learned of color in museum halls
stretched on the canvas of men not born on an island
I learned of birds that I am not the gull,
of fish that I am not the dead food
for our mouths, that flocks drink water
that's not sealed in wells. Looking in a picture
at a horse overthrowing the horseman
I grasped the limit of the stone
and for the squandering of a flower
scattered over a table I cried out as if smitten.
How much of what the eye saw
has turned to heart and hands?
Little, if I read in my book:
this also was set down recalling
all I hate: I was born on an island.
I do not forget that island.

(JP &MGT)

Adriano Spatola

BOOMERANG

1

the weapon that boomerangs, the fish is harpooned in the belly
in waves of champagne

and: prepared for a banquet and: glittering — crystal — and
i return (in a white coat) to remove the crumbs

all of us so well-fixed, naked, on the grass, for the souvenir-
photo

resolving to love each other to the point of death, suicide: the
procedure decided by telephone

the promissory-note we have endorsed with each other, now pro-
tested

shining folds, fat: blue gleam, the melting establishment

ripe fruit the suspended elevator and like the worm in the
apple here i sit inside beating out spondees

2

i earn my pay lounging in the bath for two hours, writing
gallant verses for old dowagers

but these good-for-nothings invade the squares, ruin the
paving, soak themselves with water from the hydrants

i go to buy an aperitif — an ice, perhaps — in the middle
of my race, in the middle of my people

but these good-for-nothings invade the squares, ruin the
paving, soak themselves with water from the hydrants

here with a calm wave of my hand i stop a taxi: with it i go off

but these good-for-nothings invade the squares, ruin the
paving, soak themselves with water from the hydrants

and another who by now has known them all, even those in
civilian dress, they have trampled on him: especially on
his card-carrying eyes

3

necropolis of the dodge, of wheelbarrows, of gutted trellises,
of garden-trailers in which grass grows in the rain

necropolis: death-rubble the dump-truck unloads on the river
bank, grave-debris the flood wears away and washes to the sea

when the mixer turns — sand, gravel and cement — in the
square excavated for the foundation six feet below street-level,
above the living flesh of the city

and in the cellar the family's tomb for typewriters, shelves
crowded with urns on which dust falls from the new models

but under the shed, on the construction site, the necropolis
of bicycles — blind handlebars, seats

with the raking bulldozer that uproots the lettuce in the gardens, on the terrace geraniums in a vase trampled by the man
at the antenna

parking necropolis: to visit it during the slow waning of all
souls' day, in the fog, november, dim headlights, illegible
headstones

the dates of N and M are lit and die out, flickering troubled
intensity   ·

4

ah! that thing digging in the street, the dental drill
and right inside the tooth-cavity the nicotine settles
benzolic secretions, metanephric sweats

and under the epidermis roots the arabesque of branches that
pump pus from the depths, that return the dross of the refined
oil — exhaust gas that colors the blood

christ! i just want to see them float, on the eely rippling
of the pond: spit, rotting carcasses: while i shatter

(LV)

THE COMPOSITION OF THE TEXT

1

an adjective is the breath or the opened window
the exact size of the graft in the rustling of the page
or else see how the text employs the body
see how the work is cosmic biological and logical
in the nocturnal voices in the auroral outbursts
in the crackling scratching planing or lighting
here beneath the pasty sky that dirties the fingers
words that speak

2

to the night is applied the ban on relaxing
at the window or existence is the circle is the space
the rhythmic swinging of the hook that grazes the lips
and the bronze gestures the dark room the sign left by water
framed cold face hypocritical dust hypnosis
see but see how negation modifies the text
with possible words with impossible words

3

but the text is a living object equipped with keys
the crude resection its effect the incredible osmosis
this is the moment that you await that begins to cut
see how it stretches and swells to the point of bursting
it is the immature anaconda it bites its dragging tail
the odor of the marsh the odor issued from the mud's stench
give me a book notebook pen painless desire
without words

4

and wearily now it becomes aware of its own intentions
it is not difficult to make several trials several inquiries
improbable preparations for a journey now certain
you also — let yourself become sterile don't open the door
intractable eczema spangled flesh the ruins the slaughter
in the text everything accumulates everything turns to vapor
remember it's late remember it's time to go to say goodbye
with a few precise innocuous words

5

after the first blows the material becomes insensitive
or sensitive uncertain personal risky privileged decline
in terms of organic functions and dysfunctions
or else in terms of gaping clumsy monodic choices
at this point see how the text begins to swing wild
the blow is from the rejection you leave with the same rejection
           as before
but you will take any task assigned to you
for which words are unnecessary

6

it is incoherent vague its illness is pointless
now that we are in the text densities seem to yield
a substantive is an access of coughing the beginning of hysteria
the vulgar dilation the bloody slice

without falcons without promises without hunting horns without
             catharsis
the woods are full of fragile docile stupid victims
the woods are full of love and how love hates
this word

                            7

soon the final part will begin in the text
catalogue of mannerisms and of rapes canzone and narcosis
pencilling the delivery date on the calendar
a word is the parasite the narcissus the subcutaneous rage
but see how the machine chews and foams and grows hot
the music rises the hand corrects the light dims
lower your head stretch out your arms don't close your eyes
erase that word

                                              (LV)

THE BLACK JEW

                            1

passers-by, sombre and stooped, oppressive: scarves shroud
their faces

how the grass of the freshly blooming garden burns and pours
out dense black smoke

within which the lady who slips in the wind played girl

holding her newly patched-up head very tightly with her hand

so a gust stronger than the others would not send her tumbling
over and over in the middle of the square

lady solomé ask your father only for your head

2

holding hands encircling the army tank from which we were born
we dance

seeing myself finally ascend, clambering, toward the rope
stretched tautly over space

monkey in overalls, dancing up there protected by a net formed
by the intertwined fingers of those standing below

and someone passing around a small plate, collecting change

what can i do in this mechanism mixing my time vertically

holding the pages of the book of the dead at a distance:
inscriptions, souvenirs, which i reread at night

but the destruction of a portion is finished: now, come with
me, bend down, look, touch, cracked skin

sitting at the table drinking coffee consulting the newspapers:
rain that beats on the roofs of the parked cars

perfectly tranquil, sitting in the place reserved for me, un-
mistakably, in the place booked for me

warped wreck, carrion of the ship dismantled by fish

and inside the glass case antique worms — whose progresses and
returns are followed — are arranged in a new order

3

they could tell from the flowers from the time when they
thrust out from the common graves

soft carpet of a thousand colors, colonies of worms, troops
mobilized to the front

trees sprouted exactly in the middle: above the net, intertwined fingers of those standing below

orpheus! someone says to him, erpheus! shouting, ephreus! stomping on his face, jew! then he says to him: "sing!"

sing! wake these dead people

and the wind among the leaves, air conditioned, deodorant sprayed in the bedroom

and above the net here i am dancing, singing, playing the lyre: monkey in overalls, overalls swollen with wind, pig bladder

and here i am a truck, headed straight for the open sea, sails unfurled: rock bent on drowning

pig bladder swollen with cadaverous gas, one day and already full of lard

4

stop up my nose, solder my ears, close my asshole, cement inside my mouth

carry me open-eyed through the lit city

(trees all around, no one on the street)

then, all of a sudden, on the right: a violent carnival

these people who run limping toward the empty taxis shaking banknotes

the empty taxis sliding away without stopping

these people who take embalmed cupids from the niches

sewers vomiting continually, black liquid inside shoes

5

useless to destroy the papers, useless to burn the documents

they come outside in procession, wary and patient, hidden by ragged uniforms

hands soiled with earth, pockets ripped open

and the sound of violins accompanies them all to the tram, to take the last trip

pack them in! pack them in!

block the windows, seal the doors with lead

vehicle journeying through the city day and night, recognizable noise, hobbling tram

(LV)

Maria Luisa Spaziani

JOURNEY IN THE ORIENT

Now in my Samarkand of blue enamels
the domes shine with icy winter lights.
The grain's scent sleeps; old men with gold teeth
pull turbans down over their ears.

The flies grant a respite to the bazaar donkeys,
I would no longer hear them bray their childish complaints.
Tamerlane's mulberry-trees sleep, sleep,
the huge sextant of Ulugh Beg fails to pierce the fog.

I have truly traversed the route of the Pamir;
did my dancing body leave my shadow's imprint there?
Have I breathed the incense of the caravan trails
where Bibi Khanum, the ardent one, risked his head for a glance?

The kolkoz had one wall in common with the mosque,
the leader's discourse faded in the meuzzin's cry.
I changed skin, spirit, aspect,
was nomad and fervent, seeking the traces of a god.

Now if I look at the ground I think Samarkand is down there,
separated by strata of clay, magma, and fire.
My Proserpine, inner inexpressible kernel,
point of the universe with no possible roads.

Maybe Samarkand is my own heart, the time zones
go off the rails if I try to reach it.
Samarkand goes in me; biting into fruit I illuminate it,
drinking water I nourish it, deep root.

Samarkand is the past, but so long past
that I find it sometimes in the doorway of my house,
dawn wind, star, archetype functioning in the dark,
collage with the Tartar's shout, and my mother who bakes the bread.

(RF)

TARQUINIA

I

The dead entrust little of themselves to us.
They leave us only the body, an inert
resemblance, a name, or calcined tibias
which in time the anthropologist distinguishes
with difficulty   from the bones of animals.
They leave what an abductor rips
from a fleeing girl: that is, a garment
still warm for just a few moments
from the body it covered. But descending
into the city of the dead where
an unexpressed existence is going on intact,
where soft joined beds
support the one who was loved, in a flash we see
what the dead left us: it is life,
still, and on the table set for the feast
a loaf, which thought removes from the oven,
gives off its scent
and compassion, support for human genius
like water to the leaf. This alone
is the message of the dead, their invitation
to project ourselves onto the other side, to breathe
inside an airless void,
reverse our eyes and contemplate
not growing stalk, but multiple root,
swifter than lightning.

II

Elsewhere, already not here, our meeting
was marked down by fate. You know how sparse
words were between us. Not even
our eyes expressed that flash
that seals forever a pact born
suddenly between two men. But time
in its laborious furrows, where
every fibre is transformed, (and greening

Epiphanies are turning what steeps to another
kind of fortune) that same time
has melted in glory in its forges
an instant of inert nearness.
So, between us, distant, extremely
alien as are death and life,
this bridge of liana rested
some night or other. I realize this evening
that Etruscan blood dyes the walls
of Tarquinia at sunset and in the open
a faded blue already blends
with the moon's fire. You rest
between Velca and the *lucumones,* and remind me
of those fathers the earth swallows before
their sons are born. Never, in the dark, will they
know the destiny of their seed.

(RF)

David M. Turoldo

MAN, YOUR

memories of blue dawn
move like sodden seaweed
over dead water. Your heart
— forgetful of the crowded god-
hours — stings you: and you hunt
your soul with a
parched throat.
At your window
you gnaw the wax with white teeth
and bitter flesh fences you in;
below, the water mirrors you,
enigma of conscious matter
and are only
an immense moment.

(SR)

PAUSE OF THE BLOOD

Now from a dead dawn at the start
of a road through murky night
exactly like me, naked
you follow,
you cover me with monstrous wings:
"I do this to keep you from falling"
you say with the honed teeth of a hyena,
not knowing your eyehole is an abyss.
You don't see it; our step
is fatal.
Gulleys of rotting bones and flesh
lie on the way.
You wear skulls and a noose
and smile calmly:
your smile will stop my
blood cold.

(SR)

MY NATURE

It's my nature to be
present: to love
the reality I feel: to touch,
become these dying things
save them with my com-
passionate gesture. My saddest
pleasure in these possessions
always scattered: these non-
existences: love for houses
I must leave; for this
lost city of mine.

(SR)

TEMPTED

But I'm tempted
each time I sense the light
perch on the balcony
like a swallow.
This
irrational existence,
this patch of sky
that's left to me between the houses,
these forsaken stones
are all my occasions;
memory,
where I make an appointment:
there at last I feel
I've overcome my
loneliness.

(SR)

Carlo Villa

LITTLE HORSE AT DAWN

Mountains turning to a skeleton
spin in the smoky sky,

and thrown off-track in the blast,
the earth tries its weighted flights

by rules not tested yet.
Giraffes shorten their necks,

the rhinoceros frightens no one now,
and, its martial trumpet missing,

the elephant is no bigger than a rabbit.
The horse, shrunken

to the semblance of a fox terrier
is easy prey for seals,

and will the grey of films
still be feasible? The dense mine

of reds, the ancient physics
of white, the tough mother

of black? Will the river of commas
be possible now,

the rain of accent marks,
the din of double consonants,

if the world should begin again?

(KJ)

EXEMPLARY TORTOISE

I believe in the existence of baby tortoises
travelling in a mother ship, or escaped,
but seriously injured in their wanderings,

and I have always searched for these missing babies,
maimed survivors, since:
one-eyed, limping, or armless,

they must certainly be hiding out: real true
baby excrement at the zenith
of the hell of this maternal body

of the exemplary tortoise that expels them
once they're finished and wounds them
in doing this, because of the terrible conditions there.

(KJ)

Cesare Vivaldi

MOTHER, I WON'T FORGET

Mother, I haven't forgotten you who told
me that "the wind was born
in the mountains and came down to the sea;
you were born with the wind." It was

cold, a cold October: there was a big
window behind the bed; the wind battered it,
and endless white clouds. Tell me
if you died in the wind! My heart

has run with the wind too much. I find your face
in the sea and I know that you are dead.
I find your heart, bitter and sweet, in these bitter

grape seeds, and your endless hands
in the clouds, and (I know you are dead)
the diamond of a teardrop in my heart.

(LS)

TO GIOVANNI

The sea is as green as you paint it,
and in the morning, if the weather's nice,
there are shouts of leaping boys in the cool air,
and they seem to fly, seagulls with clear voices.

You're right: the fish, the boats, the houses,
and even the strain which torments the rocks,
the wind of misery that has filled them
with bright colors which cleave your eyes.

Your world is honest, clean. In the evening
the men sit in a row with canes in hand,
a boy eating an apple watches them,
and a coal boat passes in the distance.

(LS)

Paolo Volponi

ANOTHER VOICE

1

Even if the song
of the girl who drives
the crows from the backs
of the oxen is sad,
it's easy to linger
at the rims of the caves,
to yield to the falcon's calls,
to deceive yourself that you've found
the wolves' den;
the long snow
treats me to a cabin,
to the sweet smells
of acorns and chestnuts.
Lethargy brings oracles.

2

When in the moon's mirror
the stream filters
through the fragrant bushes
and the ring of trenches
is full
and my horse
wanders freely;

when the graveyards of ancient wars
surface at the mountain passes
and the canebrake turns traitor
at the stream's mouth;

and the skylark trembles
among the stones
naked and bright
as the breast of a bride,

in my beloved field
the oxherd girl
will have another voice—
like a quail song.

(LS)

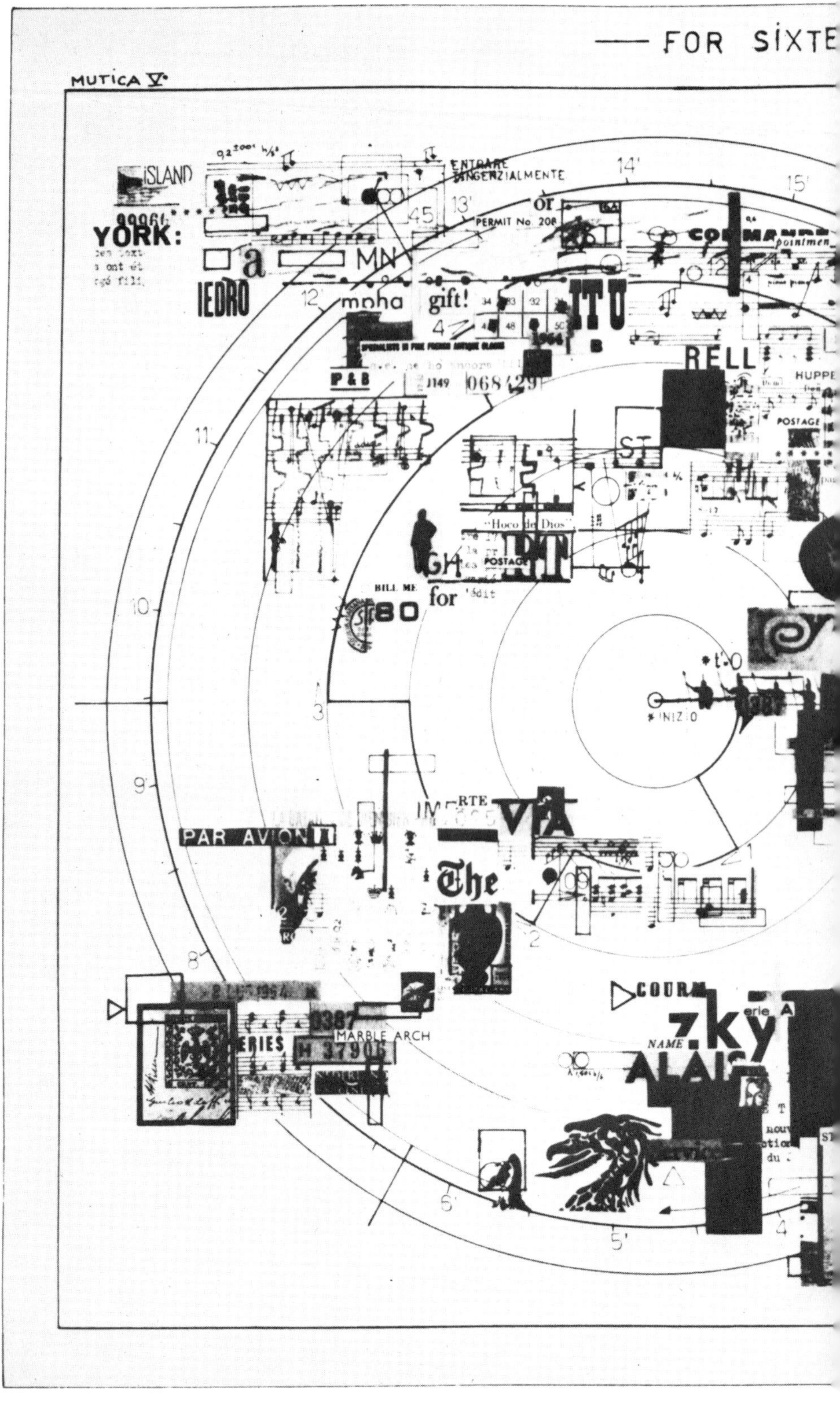
— FOR SIXTE
MUTICA V
ISLAND
YORK:
IEDRO
ENTRARE
TANGENZIALMENTE
PERMIT No. 208
MN
gift!
RELL
HUPPE
POSTAGE
P & B
068429
ST
"Hoco de Dios"
POSTAGE
BILL ME
for
80
INIZIO
PAR AVION
RTE
VIA
The
COURM
NAME
ALAIS
MARBLE ARCH
3387
SERIES

RCHES 1964

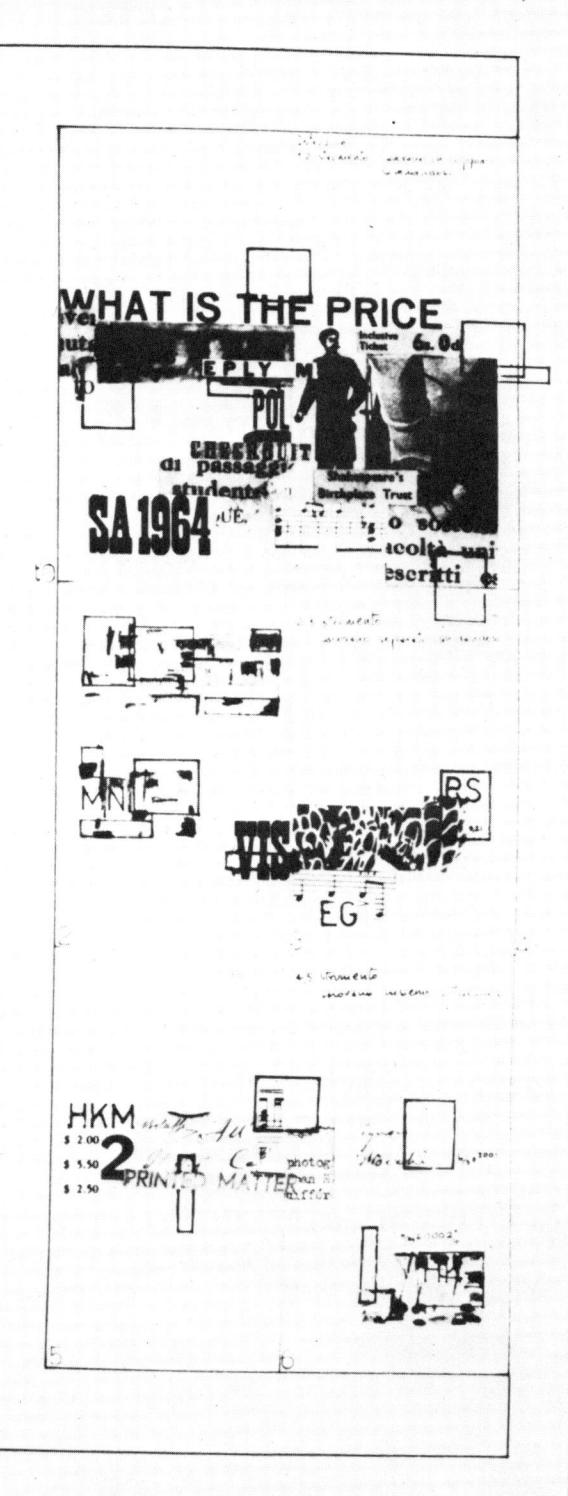

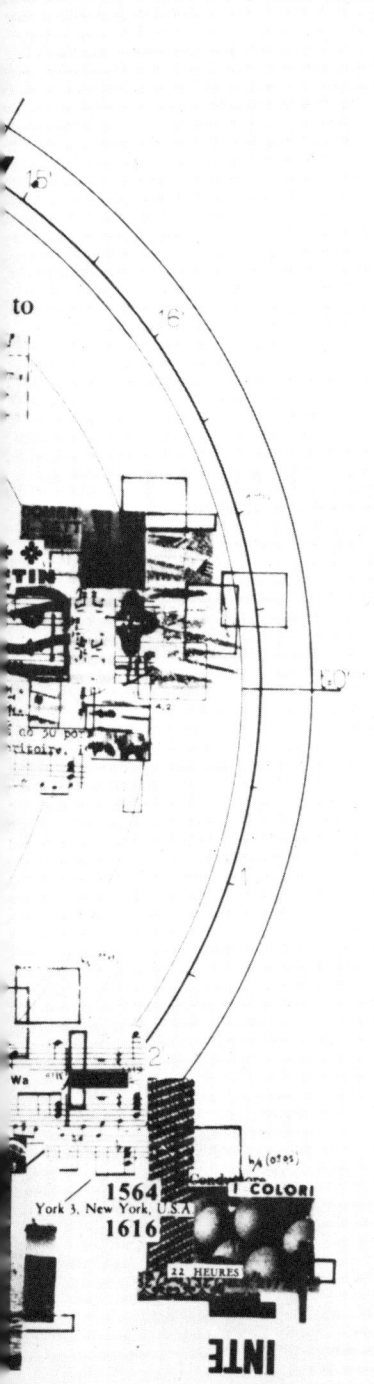

NOTES

GENOVESE, "Anamnesis", line 44, 'Adamites':
The *Adamites* were followers of a heresy current in the second century A.D., which was revived in the fifteenth. It advocated the promiscuity of sexes, practised total nudity, and taught that carnal sins were a sign of higher spirituality.

LUNETTA, "In Respect of Tradition", line 11, 'seventese': a *serventese* is a poetic composition of Provençal origin.

OMBRES, "Bella and the Golem", note by the author:

> Bella is related, so to speak, to the angel Raziel: he knows the secret names and she knows how to read the Name with the right 'pronunciation'. But clearly she is related also to the young princess from Andersen's tale *'The Wild Swans'*. There the young princess weaves nettles to make tunics in order to save her brothers, and Bella too works to save. This golem, more than the golem that sparked debate among the mystics, is the golem of the legend that has as its protagonist Yehudah Low Bezalcel, who lived in Prague toward the end of the 16th Century. It is legend based on the thaumaturgy of the Tetragrammaton: the golem's creator forgets once to take away from him his Name and thus, afraid that he might become dangerous, pursues and destroys him.
>
> Naturally, the city where my golem moves is the Prague of Gustav Meyrink that Kafka loved so much. However the golem of this story is destroyed by a woman, who deprives him of his life-giving letters by 'reading' them in a particular way that will deprive the monstrous robot of his vital energy. Since I was a child, I have always thought that monsters could be vanquished by women.
>
> 'Whoever has a yod in his name': according to a Talmudic hypothesis, the world of the future is created with this small letter.

ORELLI, "Sinopie", title:
Sinopie are the reddish-brown drawings executed on wet plaster as guides for the subsequent frescoes.

SPAZIANI, "Tarquinia", II, line 21, 'lucumones':
The *lucumones* were Etruscan nobles who possessed both priestly and princely powers.

BIOGRAPHICAL NOTES ON THE POETS

Nanni Balestrini was born in Milan in 1935. He is editor of *Il Verri*, has experimented with taped and electronic music, and translated extensively from contemporary German poetry. A ballet he wrote was performed at La Scala. His more recent collections of poems are: *Altri procedimenti* (1966) and *Ma noi facciamone un'altra* (1968).

Luigi Ballerini was born in Milan in 1940 and now teaches Italian Literature at New York University. He has translated a number of books into Italian and published *eccetera. E* (poetry 1972) and *La piramide capovolta* (essays, 1975). He is founder of Out of London Press. A book of poetic texts and a book of essays are forthcoming.

Dario Bellezza was born in 1944 in Rome and has always lived there. He began publishing in *Nuovi Argomenti* and continued in other literary journals. Among his books are an epistolary novel and one in verse form, a novel entitled *Il figlio prodigo,* and two volumes of poetry: *Invettive e licenze* (1971) and *Morte segreta* (1976).

Piero Bigongiari was born in Pisa in 1914, and is presently Professor of Modern and Contemporary Italian Literature at the Facoltà di Magistero of Florence. His collections of poetry include *La figlia di Babilonia* (1942), *Il corvo bianco* (1955), *Torre de Arnolfo* (1964), *Stato di cose* (1968) and the forthcoming *Moses.*

Alfredo Bonazzi was born in Altripalda in 1929. After the war he gravitated to a life of crime, and was convicted of murder in Milan. In 1965 he began writing poetry in jail. Three years later *Annunciazione* was published. Three more books have followed, and an autobiography. In 1973 he received a pardon.

Edith Bruck was born in 1932 in the Hungarian village of Tizabércel. The whole family was deported to Germany, where she survived a concentration camp. She has lived and written in Italy for a number of years, and has published short stories, novellas, and novels. She published her first book of poems in 1975.

Ferdinando Camon was born in 1935 near Padova. He has published fiction and one book of poems, *Fuori storia* (1967).

Giorgio Caproni was born in Livorno in 1912. He is the author of ten books of poems, the latest of which is *Il muro della terra* (1975). He has translated Apollinaire, Baudelaire, Céline, Char, Frénaud, Genêt, Proust.

Giovanni Cecchetti was born in Pescia, Tuscany, and educated at the University of Florence. He has organized centers of Italian studies at various American universities, the latest being UCLA. He is the author of numerous essays, has translated Verga, and written two books of criticism. He has also published two books of poems.

Guido Ceronetti was born in Piedmont in 1927. He has translated Martial and Catullus, and the Old Testament Psalms. The book from which our translations are made is *Poesie/Frammenti/Poesie Separate* (1968).

Giorgio Chiesura was born in Venice in 1921. He did not publish until *Non scrivete il mio nome* in 1957. It was followed by *Sicilia '43* and *La zona immobile* in 1969.

Pietro Cimatti was born in Forlì in 1929. He has edited *Fiera Letteraria* and is the author of six books of poems, of which the most recent is *Assolutamente fuori* (1971). He has also translated and edited a volume of Nicaraguan "politico-poetical" writing, *Nicaragua ora zero* (1970). He now lives in Rome and writes for *Il Messagero.*

Elena Clementelli was born in Rome in 1923 and works at the Italo-Latin American Institute there. In addition to four volumes of her own verse, she has published translations, including an anthology of Blues and another of Negro Spirituals in collaboration with Walter Mauro.

Roberto Coppini was born in Florence in 1927. The only collection of his poetry that has been published is *Swimming Pool* (1968 — English title).

Raffaele Crovi was born in 1934 at Paderno Dugnano (Milan). The latest of his five books of poems is *Genesi* (1974).

Maurizio Cucchi, born in Milan in 1945, published a volume of his own poetry, *Paradossalmente e con affanno,* in 1970. His poetry has appeared in the magazines *Paragone* and *Nuovi Argomenti,* and a new book, *Il disperso,* came out in 1976 at Mondadori.

Brandolino Brandolini d'Adda was born in 1928, and has published four books of poetry, including *Otto spartiti* (1977). He lives in Milan where he is the Managing Director of the Italian *Reader's Digest.*

Milo De Angelis was born in Milan in 1951, and has published poetry in various magazines.

Alfredo de Palchi was born near Verona. After some years in France and Spain, he came to the U.S. in the late fifties. His work appeared in many magazines and anthologies. His book *Sessioni con l'analista* (1967) appeared in English in 1970 as *Sessions With My Analyst* (tr. I.L. Salomon).

Arnaldo Di Benedetto was born in 1940 at Malles Venosta (Bolzano). He teaches Italian language and literature at the University of Turin. He has not yet published a book of poems.

Luciano Erba was born in Milan in 1922. He now teaches French Literature at the University of Verona. His books include *Linea K* (1951), *Il bel paese* (1955), *Il prete de Ratana* (1959), and *Il male minore* (1960).

Elizabeth Ferrero was born in Turin, Italy, where she was raised. She has taught Italian at LaGuardia Community College, New York, for the past three years, and has been published in Italy and America in *La Fusta, Zone One, Invisible City, Junction, Tam Tam.*

Gilberto Finzi was born in Mantua in 1927 and now lives in Milan. He has authored two books of criticism as well as the following books of poetry: *Milano la sera de Cuba* (1963), *La nuova arca* (1965), and *L'Alto medioevo nel suo più brutale ricorso ai nostri giorni* (1971).

Andrea Genovese was born in Messina in 1937. He has lived and worked in Milan since 1960. Active politically, he was a candidate for Parliament in 1970. His three books of poetry are: *Odissea minima* (1964), *Sexantropus* (1976), and *Bestiario* (1977).

Amedeo Giacomini was born in Varmo in 1940 and now works in Udine. As well as translations from the French, he has published a novel and the following two volumes of poetry: *La vita artificiale* (1968) and *Incostanza de Narciso* (1973).

Alfredo Giulliani was born in Pesaro in 1924. He has translated Dylan Thomas, Joyce, William Empson, and E.A. Robinson. He has published a book of essays and edited several anthologies, including *I novissimi.* His most recent books of poems are *Povera Juliet e altre poesie* (1965), and *Chi l'avrebbe detto* (1973).

Renato Gorgoni was born in Naples in 1927. He has published poems in various journals: *Il bimestre, L'erba voglio, Linus*.

Margherita Guidacci was born in Florence in 1927. She has published four books of poetry, including *Paglia e polvere* (1961) and *Poesie* (1965).

Armanda Guiducci was born in Naples, and is known as critic and travel writer as well as poet. Her book of poems, *Poesie per un uomo*, came out in 1965.

Federico Hinderman was born in Biella in 1921 of a Swiss father and Italian mother. He has published a book of poems in German (in 1940). Poems of his in Italian have appeared in the *Neue Zürcher Zeitung*.

Gina Labriola was born in the Lucania region of Southern Italy. Her first book of poetry was *Istante d'amore ibernato* (1972), and her second is *Alveare di specchi* (1974). She has lived in Iran, and now lives in Spain.

Mario Lunetta was born in Rome in 1934. He has published a short novel, a collection of essays, a monograph on Svevo and two books of poetry, *Tredici falchi* (1970) and *Lo stuzzicadenti di Jarry* (1972).

Georgio Luzzi: unfortunately we have no information

Giancarlo Majorino was born in Milan in 1928, where he still lives. He is the editor of *Il Corpo* and one of the poetry editors of *Il paragone*. His first book of poems was *La capitale del nord* (1959), and his latest *Equilibrio in pezzi* (1971).

Giorgio Manacorda was born in Rome in 1941. He has published frequently in major Italian journals and written for a number of newspapers, often about German literature. His latest book is *Iconografia* (1974).

Giorgio Mannacio was born in 1932 at San Nicolà da Crissa (Catanzaro). He has published his poetry in *Il Caffè* and *Almanacco dello specchio*.

Dacia Maraini was born in Florence in 1936. She spent the first eight years of her life in Japan, some of them in a concentration camp with her father. She now lives in Rome, where she is an active feminist. She has written novels, stories, and plays. Her two books of poetry are *Crudeltà all'aria aperta* (1966) and *Donne mie* (1974).

Elsa Morante was born in Rome in 1918. She has published collections of short stories and fables, as well as the well-known novels *Menzogna e sortilegio* (1948) and *L'isola di Arturo* (1957). She has also written poetry, and her latest book of poems is *Il mondo salvato dai ragazzini* (1968). Her most recent novel is *La storia* (1974).

Alberto Moriconi was born in Terni (Umbria) in 1910, and now lives in Naples, where he writes a weekly column for the literary page of *Il Mattino*. He has written plays, articles, and five books of poetry, the latest of which is *Un carico di Mercurio* (1975).

Giampiero Neri is a pen-name for Giuseppe Pontiggia who was born in Erbe in 1927. His poems have appeared in the magazine *Il Corpo* and in a volume published in 1976 under the title *L'aspetto occidentale del vestito*.

Giulia Niccolai was born in Milan. She has published a novel, *Il grande angolo* (1966), and her collections of poetry include *Humpty Dumpty* (1969), *Greenwich* (1971), and *Poema & oggetto* (1975). With Adriano Spatola she edits *Tam Tam*.

Stanislao Nievo was born in Milan in 1928. He is preparing his first book of poems for publication.

Rossana Ombres was born in Turin and now lives in Rome. Her books of poems are *Orizzonte anche tu* (1956), *Le ciminiere di Casale* (1962), *L'ipotesi di Agar* (1968) and *Bestiario d'amore* (1974). In 1970 she published her first novel, *Principessa Giacinta*. In 1977 she published another novel, *Memorie di una dilettante*.

Giorgio Orelli was born in Airolo (Canton Ticino) in 1921. He has published six volumes of poetry, including *Nel cerchio familiare* (1960), *L'ora del tempo* (1962), and *6 Poesie* (1964).

Elio Pagliarani was born in Viserba in 1927. He was a member of the avant-garde group *I novissimi*, and has published *Cronache e altre poesie* (1954), *Inventario privato* (1959) and *La ragazza Carla e altre poesie* (1962).

Pier Paolo Pasolini was born in Bologna in 1922, and was murdered in Rome in 1975. He was novelist, poet, critic, film-director. As well as poems in 'standard' Italian, he wrote in the Friulan dialect. The poems in this book are from *La nuova gioventù* (1975), which has poems in Friulan written between 1941 and 1974.

Camillo Pennati was born in Milan in 1931 and lived for many years in London. He has translated Thom Gunn, Philip Larkin, and Ted Hughes. His latest book of poetry is *Erosagonie* (1973).

Alessandro Peregalli was born in Milan in 1923. He is the author of *L'Altopiano* (1955) and the recent *Cronaca*.

Danilo Plateo: unfortunately we have no information

Antonio Porta was born in Milan in 1932, and has published the following books of poems: *La palpebra rovesciata* (1960), *Zero* (1963), *Aprire* (1964), *I rapporti* (1965), *Cara* (1969), and *Metropolis* (1971).

Vasco Pratolini is one of Italy's leading novelists. He grew up in Florence, and in the 1940's was a member of the Resistance. His best-known works are *Il quartiere* (1944), *Cronaca familiare* and *Cronache di poveri amanti* (both 1947), *La costanza della ragione* (1963) and the trilogy *Metello, Lo scialo, allegoria e derisione* (1955-66). He has started to publish poetry only recently.

Giovanni Raboni was born in Milan in 1932. He has published the following books of poems: *Il catalogo é questo* (1961), *L'insalubrità dell'aria (1963), Le case della Vetra* (1966), *L'intoppo* (1967), and *Economia della paura* (1970).

Silvio Ramat was born in Florence in 1939 and teaches modern and contemporary Italian literature at the University of Padova. In addition to five collections of verse, he has published critical works on hermeticism and other aspects of twentieth-century Italian poetry.

Franco Rella: unfortunately we have no information.

Nelo Risi was born in Milan in 1920 and now lives in Rome. He is a well-known film-maker. His most important volumes of poetry are: *Polso teso* (1956), *Pensieri elementari* (1961), *Dentro la sostanza* (1965), *Di certe cose* (1970), *Amica mia nemica* (1976).

Roberto Roversi was born in 1923 in Bologna, where he still lives. He was a partisan in the war and in 1955 began the important magazine *Officina*. He has published nine books of poems, the latest of which is *I diecimila cavalli* (1976).

Sergio Salvi was born in Florence in 1932. He has published four books of poems, the latest of which is *Le croci di Cartesio* (1966). He has also published a prose narrative *L'oro del Rodano*. He is employed by the government of his native city.

Giovanna Sandri was born in Rome, where she still lives. Her works of *poesia visiva* have been widely exhibited, and her poems have appeared in many magazines. She has published a book, *Capitolo zero* (1969), and her *From K to S (Ark of the Aysmmetric)* was published by Out Of London Press in 1976.

Roberto Sanesi was born in Milan in 1930. He is a literary critic specializing in English literature. He has written for the theater and translated a number of poets, including Thomas, Yeats, and Eliot, as well as edited a number of anthologies of English poetry. His latest book of poems is *Alterego e altre ipotesi* (1974).

Born in Genova in 1930, Edoardo Sanguineti currently teaches Italian literature at the University of Salerno. He has written books on Dante, Moravia, and Gozzano, as well as plays, and three novels. He has written four books of poetry, the most recent being *Wirrwarr* (1972).

Francesco Smeraldi, born in Venice in 1942, published a collection of his poetry, *Una ragione privata* (1968) for the *Editions Club du Poème*.

Adriano Spatola was born in Sapjane, Yugoslavia, in 1941. He co-edits the magazine *Tam-Tam*, and has published a novel, a book of essays, a poem-puzzle, *poesia da montare* (1965), a collection of concrete poems, *Zeroglifico* (1966), and three other books of poems, the latest of which is *Majakovskiiiiiiij* (1971).

Maria Luisa Spaziani was born in Turin in 1924 and now lives in Rome. She has written five books of poetry, including *L'occhio del ciclone* (1970) and *Transito con catene* (1977).

David Maria Turoldo was born in 1916 in Coderno del Friuli, and entered the Order of the Servi at 24. He has written four books of poetry, the most recent of which is *Il sesto angelo* (1976, a selection).

Carlo Villa was born in Rome in 1931. His books of poetry are: *Il privilegio di essere vivi* (1962) and *Siamo esseri vivi* (1964). He has also written fiction: *La nausea media* (1964), *Deposito celeste* (1967), *I sensi lunghi* (1970), and *L'isola in bottiglia* (1972).

Cesare Vivaldi was born in Imperia in 1925 and now lives in Rome. He was part of the Gruppo '63, and is best known as a novelist. His books of poetry include *Dialogo con l'ombra* (1960), *Poesie ligure* (1960), and *Dettagli* (1964).

Paolo Volponi was born in Urbino in 1924, and now lives in Ivrea. He holds a degree in law and works for Olivetti. His books of poetry include *L'antica moneta* (1955), and *Le porte dell' Appennino* (1960). He has also written novels.

BIOGRAPHICAL NOTES ON THE TRANSLATORS

William Alexander is Associate Professor of English at the University of Michigan. He has a book forthcoming on William Dean Howells and has translated three books of Sanesi.

Karen D. Antonelli was born in Trieste and lived in Rome until 1972. She graduated from Vassar in 1973, and is at present writing her Ph.D. dissertation at UCLA on Marinetti and Futurism.

John Ashbery has published six books of poems and co-authored a novel. Among his books are *The Double Dream of Spring* (1970) and *Three Poems* (1972). He has received many honors and awards.

Anita Barrows was born in New York City in 1947 and now lives in Berkeley. Her poetry and short stories have been published in various magazines, and she has translated fiction, non-fiction and plays from both French and Italian.

Peter Burian trained at Michigan and Princeton, and has spent three years on and off in Rome and Florence. He teaches Classics and Comparative Literature at Duke University. He is active as an interpreter and translator of Greek tragedy.

Mary Jane Ciccarello is currently a Ph.D. candidate and a teaching assistant in the Italian Department at Columbia University.

Ann Deagon teaches Classics at Guilford College. Her books of poems include: *Poetics South* (1974), *Carbon 14* (1974), *There Is No Balm in Birmingham* (1977).

W.S. Di Piero is a poet and translator. His poems have appeared in *Hudson Review, boundary 2, Southern Review,* and elsewhere. His translations have appeared in such places as *American Poetry Review* and *Canto*.

D.J. Dutschke is a Professor of Italian at the University of California, where his main area of scholarly activity is the Middle Ages. He has published articles on Petrarch and Boccaccio, translated Quasimodo, and in 1977 his book, *Francesco Petrarca: Canzone XXIII from First to Final Version,* appeared.

Dino Fabris is a writer, poet, and translator. He was born in Friuli and now lives in Massachusetts.

Rina (Caterina) Ferrarelli came to the U.S. from Italy in 1954. For the past few years she has worked as a teacher and research assistant in cross-cultural anthropology. She has published translations and poems in a number of magazines and is writing a novel.

Jonathan Galassi is a poet, critic, translator, and editor at Houghton Mifflin. He is currently translating his literary essays for publication by Ecco Press.

Marisa Gatti-Taylor was born in 1946 in the Republic of San Marino. She received her Ph.D. in Franch and Italian from Wayne State University in 1973, and has translated Pascoli.

Kathrine Jason graduated from Bard in 1975 and received her M.F.A. in poetry from Columbia in 1978. Her translations from Spanish and Italian have appeared in several magazines and anthologies.

Frank Judge has taught at SUNY/Brockport and Rochester Institute of Technology. He spent a year in Italy on a Fulbright. His poetry and translations have appeared in many journals, and he is Managing Editor of the magazine *Survivor*.

Richard H. Lansing was born in Rochester, N.Y., in 1943. He is Assistant Professor of Italian and Comparative Literature at Brandeis University. His *From Image to Idea: A Study of the Simile in Dante's Commedia* appeared in 1977.

Donold Lourie was born in Chicago in 1920. He is enrolled in the School of the Arts at Columbia University, after having worked for a number of years in a New York bank.

Charles Matz is an oral poet who has lived in Italy for many years. He teaches at the Linguistic University in Feltre.

Richard Milazzo was born in New York City in 1949. He is editor of Out of London Press and has published in *Il Verri* and *Altri termini*. He is currently editing *The Syntactic Revolution* by Abraham Lincoln Gillespie.

RoseAnna Mueller was born near Palermo in 1948 and came to the U.S. when she was six. She has a Ph.D. in Comparative Literature from CUNY. She is currently teaching in the Literature Department of The American University.

Art Neisberg was born in Chicago in 1942. He has a PhD from Brown, and is presently teaching at the University of Louisville.

Ida Nolemi is currently a Ph.D. candidate and a teaching assistant in the Italian Department at Columbia University.

Jan Pallister was born in Minnesota in 1926. She is a Professor in the Department of Romance Languages at Bowling Green State University. She is a widely published poet and translator, and has written scholarly works.

Edgar Pauk was born in Fiume in 1938 and came to the United States in 1956. He holds a degree in international law and a doctorate in Spanish literature from Yale. He now lives in New York City, where he practises law.

John Pellerzi was born near Parma, Italy, in 1950. He is presently working on his Ph.D. in Italian at N.Y.U.

Sonia Raiziss is editor of *Chelsea*. Her translations and poems have been widely published. She is author of two books of criticism and a new book of poems, *Bucks County Blues*.

Martin Robbins has published two books of his own poetry with Swallow Press. He teaches writing and editing in the Radcliffe Seminars program, and at the Harvard Extension.

Lawrence R. Smith was born in Rochester, N.Y., in 1945. He teaches modern poetry and creative writing at Eastern Michigan University, has published poetry, translations, essays, in a number of magazines, and held a Fulbright lectureship in Rome, 1973-74.

Lawrence Venuti is a doctoral candidate in English and Comparative Literature at Columbia University. His translations of modern Italian poetry have appeared in *International Poetry Review* and *Small Moon*.

John Yau has published in a number of magazines, including *Ploughshares* and *New York Arts Journal*. His book of poems is entitled *The Reading of an Ever-Changing Tale* (1976).

Ruth Feldman and Brian Swann have published *Collected Poems of Lucio Piccolo* (Princeton University Press, 1972), *Selected Poetry of Andrea Zanzotto* (Princeton U.P., 1975), and *Shema: Collected Poems of Primo Levi* (Menard Press, London), which won the John Florio Prize for the best book of Italian-English translation published in the U.K. in 1976. *The Dawn Is Always New: Selected Poems of Rocco Scotellaro,* is forthcoming from Princeton University Press.